Cuttlefish Bones

Also by Eugenio Montale

POETRY

Ossi di seppia (Cuttlefish Bones)
Le occasioni (The Occasions)
La bufera e altro (The Storm and Other Things)
Quaderno di traduzioni (Notebook of Translations)
Satura (Miscellany)
Diario del '71 e del '72 (Diary of 1971 and 1972)
Quaderno di quattro anni (Notebook of Four Years)
Tutte le poesie (Collected Poems)
L'opera in versi (Poetical Works)
Altri versi e poesie disperse (Other and Uncollected Poems)

PROSE

Farfalla di Dinard (Butterfly of Dinard)
Eugenio Montale / Italo Svevo: Lettere con gli scritti di Montale su Svevo
  (The Montale–Svevo Letters, with Montale's Writings on Svevo)
Auto da fé: Cronache in due tempi (Act of Faith: Chronicles of Two Periods)
Fuori di casa (Away from Home)
La poesia non esiste (Poetry Doesn't Exist)
Nel nostro tempo (In Our Time)
Sulla poesia (On Poetry)
Lettere a Quasimodo (Letters to Quasimodo)
Prime alla Scala (Openings at la Scala)
Quaderno genovese (Genoa Notebook)

Also by the translator, William Arrowsmith

TRANSLATIONS

The Bacchae; Cyclops; Orestes; Hecuba; and *Heracles* by Euripides
Satyricon by Petronius
Birds by Aristophanes
Clouds by Aristophanes
Dialogues with Leucò by Cesare Pavese
    (translated with D. S. Canre-Ross)
Alcestis by Euripides
Hard Labor by Cesare Pavese
That Bowling Alley on the Tiber by Michelangelo Antonioni
The Storm and Other Things by Eugenio Montale
The Occasions by Eugenio Montale

EDITORSHIPS

The Craft and Context of Translation (edited by Roger Shattuck)
Image of Italy
Six Modern Italian Novellas
The Greek Tragedies in New Translations (in thirty-three volumes,
    in process of appearance)

Cuttlefish Bones (1920–1927)

Eugenio Montale

Translated with Preface and Commentary, by

William Arrowsmith

W · W · Norton & Company
New York   London

First published as a Norton paperback 1994

Printed in the United States of America

Library of Congress Cataloging-in-Publication Data

Montale, Eugenio, 1896–
    [Ossi di seppia.   English]
    Cuttlefish bones : 1920–1927 / Eugenio Montale ; translated, with
preface and commentary by William Arrowsmith.
        p.   cm.
    I. Arrowsmith, William, 1924–   . II. Title.
PQ4829.056508313   1993
851´.912—dc20   92-41153

ISBN 0-393-31171-6

W. W. Norton & Company, Inc., 500 Fifth Avenue, New York, N.Y. 10110
W. W. Norton & Company Ltd., 10 Coptic Street, London WC1A 1PU

 2 3 4 5 6 7 8 9 0

Contents

TRANSLATOR'S PREFACE   xv

IN LIMINE

    Rejoice when the breeze . . .   3

MOVEMENTS

    The Lemon Trees   7
    English Horn   11
    Falsetto   13
    Minstrels   17

    POEMS FOR CAMILLO SBARBARO   19
        1. Café at Rapallo   19
        2. Epigram   23

    Almost a Fantasia   25

    SARCOPHAGI   27
        Where girls with wavy hair pass by . . .   27
        Walk more warily now . . .   29
        The fire crackling . . .   31
        But where is the lover's tomb . . .   33

    OTHER VERSES   35
        Wind and Banners   35
        Shoot stretching from the wall . . .   37

CUTTLEFISH BONES

Don't ask me for words . . .   41
To laze at noon . . .   43
Don't take shelter in the shade . . .   45
I think again of your smile . . .   47
What I ask, my life . . .   49
Bring me the sunflower . . .   51
I have often met . . .   53
What you knew of me . . .   55
There Triton surges . . .   57
I know that moment . . .   59
Splendor of noon outspread . . .   61
Happiness won . . .   63
Again the canebrake . . .   65
Maybe one morning . . .   67
Valmorbia . . .   69
Your hand was trying . . .   71
The children's farandole . . .   73
Faint wind-borne sistrum . . .   75
The windlass creaks . . .   77
Haul your paper boats . . .   79
Hoopoe, merry bird . . .   81
Above the graffiti-covered wall . . .   83

MEDITERRANEAN

A squall . . .   87
O Ancient, I am drunk . . .   89
At times, climbing down . . .   91
I have lingered . . .   93
Suddenly, at times . . .   95
What tomorrow will bring . . .   97
I would have liked to feel rough . . .   99
If only I could force . . .   101
Squander, if you want . . .   103

NOONS AND SHADOWS

I
End of Childhood   107

AGAVE ON THE CLIFF   115
   O scirocco, rabid gale . . .   115
   And now they're gone . . .   117
   Now the calm returns . . .   119

Pool   121
Eclogue   123
Flux   127
Slope   131

II
Arsenio   135

III
Chrysalis   139
Moiré   145
House by the Sea   151
The Dead   155
Delta   159
Encounter   161

SEACOASTS

   Seacoasts . . .   167

NOTES AND COMMENTARY   171

Editor's Note

When William Arrowsmith died on February 20, 1992, he left in manuscript his translations of every volume of poems by Eugenio Montale arranged by the poet himself, except for *The Storm and Other Things (La bufera e altro)* and *The Occasions (Le occasioni),* which had already appeared from Norton in W. A.'s translation. *Altri versi,* put together for Montale by Giorgio Zampa and published a few months before the poet's death in 1981, was not included. In preparing *Cuttlefish Bones (Ossi di seppia)* for publication, my task has been to check the poems and notes for typing errors and inconsistencies, and, with the help of Carrol Hassman, to piece together W. A.'s preface from his drafts. The preface was the only part of the book he had not completed; the reader will find that the final paragraphs have a rough texture, since they are composed of jottings found among W. A.'s Montale papers. The prose is his, but it is the private prose of a translator/scholar setting down material to be shaped later.

In editing the book, I have relied on the invaluable advice of Claire de C. L. Huffman, Stanley Burnshaw, and Christopher Ricks, and on the dedication and patience of W. A.'s assistant, Carrol Hassman.

The initials "R. W." indicate a footnote by Rosanna Warren; the initials "C. H." indicate Claire Huffman.

Rosanna Warren

Translator's Preface

Cuttlefish Bones (Ossi di seppia) appeared in 1925, when Montale was twenty-nine. Born in Genoa in 1896 of fairly affluent parents (his father Domingo was an importer of marine paints), he attended school in Genoa, receiving his degree in accounting in 1915, but because of poor health he was often absent from class. It was his sister, Marianna, a philosophy student two years older than Montale, who guided his real education, giving him Saint Augustine, Pascal, Schopenhauer, Nietzsche, and spending long hours in intimate discussion. When he was nine, his father built a summer villa at Monterosso, one of the five small towns (the Cinque Terre) lying on the Ligurian coast just west of La Spezia. This harsh, rocky, sun-stricken edge of Mediterranean coast provided the poet at an impressionable age with a mythical sea- and landscape of his own, that "geography of the soul," both physical and metaphysical, so crucial to Montale throughout his life but above all to the poet of *Cuttlefish Bones.* "It's odd to think," Montale wrote later of his Liguria, "that each of us has a countryside like this, however different, which must always remain *his* landscape, unchanging; it's odd that the natural flow of things is so slow to seep into us and then so impossible to eradicate." From his tenth year to his thirtieth, Montale spent every summer at Monterosso. And as the Ligurian landscape gradually interiorized itself, making its way into his emotions and bloodstream, with the passing of the years the emotions in turn blooded his mind and became poetic thought.

His education continued into the summer in the company of Marianna and the culturally ambitious family of cousin Domenico, who shared the house, with Sunday visits from Marianna's philosophy teacher, a "modernist" Barnabite priest locally suspected of shocking heresies. "Sentimental education" was provided by long, solitary walks of exploration along the shore and up the steep slopes, through brush, boulders, and canebrake—an education in natural history, spent in watching birds and fauna, plants, winds, and weather, studying the world and naming it with that precision so evident in the *Ossi.* But Liguria was also a lonely, privileged, and cramping world, exempting the young Montale from growing and ripening, imprisoning him in too straitened a parish of reality. Later, while acknowledging that his Ligurian years were extremely important in his development, he observed that they also led "to introversion, to an imprisonment in the cosmos." And it was to escape this parochial world of what amounted to an extended childhood that in 1927, doubtless with a sense of enterprise, decisiveness, excitement, and relief, he left Liguria and Genoa for Florence:

> I repeat, this period [in Liguria] was an extremely formative one. But as regards cultural growth, the twenty years I spent in Florence were the most important of my life. It was there that I discovered that, besides the sea, there is also *terra firma*—the *terra firma* of ideas, tradition, humanism. There I found a different nature, one that suffused man's worth and thought. It was there that I learned what civilization has been and can be. . . .[1]

But though successive, these life stages are for Montale anything but discontinuous. Liguria is not, could not be, abandoned. The two regions and stages continue to interpenetrate as ideal polar geographies: country and city; child and man; province and capital; emotion and intellect; summer and winter; poetry and non-poetry (an Italian critical distinction, to be used cautiously). Between their polarities the poet shuffles back and forth, correcting for balance as personal and / or poetic needs dictate. When the city becomes oppressive ("noisy cities where the sky is nothing / but patches of blue . . . between the cornices . . . / the tedium of winter thickens. / The light grows niggardly, the soul bitter."—"The Lemon Trees"), the poet is drawn to the reality or memory of an ideal, idyllic Liguria, to the old miracle of light, and silence and ignorance (see, for instance, *"There Triton surges . . ."* and *"Your hand was trying . . ."*), from which, presumably refreshed, he returns to the life of work, commitment, and human solidarity.

The two regions, as well as the subordinate polar terms, are dialectically related, mutually reinforcing. "All my poetry," Montale once said, "is a waiting for the miracle." But the miracle requires the non-miracle in order to occur; the emergence of poetry requires its antecedent absence; the light requires a darkness to dispel; Liguria posits a Florence, and so on. The poet Pascoli had theorized that every true poet is inherently a child, a *puer,* that without the child there can be no poetry. To which Montale assented, adding, however, that the child must be partnered by

[1] *"Intenzioni (Intervista immaginaria),"* La Rassegna d'Italia, vol. 1, no. 1 (January 1946), 84–9; reprinted in Sulla Poesia (Milan, 1976), 561–69.

the man; if not, the poet would be incomplete, merely puerile. The Ligurian regionalist poets—Boine, Ceccardi, and even his friend Camillo Sbarbaro (see notes on "Poems for Camillo Sbarbaro"), had in his opinion honored "the child within" to the exclusion of the man. By so doing, they had chosen safety and, by renouncing both Italy and Europe, remained literarily provincial and poetic children. By leaving Liguria for Florence in 1927 (and later Milan), Montale had quite consciously decided (always a key event for the indecisive Montale) to take the exhilarating risk of beating out his own Italian and European destiny as man and poet.

But this is to anticipate. Like many adolescents, Montale wrote poetry, mostly humorous satirical "grotesques." But he said that he lacked as a boy

> . . . any instruction in poetry or any desire to "specialize" in that sense. In those years almost nobody cared about poetry. The last success I recall in those days was Gozzano, but the severer sort disparaged him, and I too (wrongly) shared their opinion. The better literary men . . . thought that, from then on, poetry should be written in prose. . . .[2]

Music, not poetry, was Montale's early passion. And instead of attending the university, for years he devoted himself to becoming a professional opera singer. His teacher, the baritone Ernesto Sivori, regarded him as extremely promising. But Sivori's death in 1923 and his father's opposition to a singer's career caused him to abandon his plans. Besides, he realized that life as a singer meant single-minded and exclusive concentration on music. "And I had other interests," he noted. "And maybe I wasn't so dumb: to be a good singer requires a mixture of originality [genialità] and stupidity." In any case, even before Sivori's death, he was spurred on to the service of poetry, a less demanding Muse. By the age of twenty, he had already produced one of his most famous poems, "Lazing at Noon . . ." ("Meriggiare pallido e assorto").[3]

Such precocity, however, was unique in Montale's oeuvre, as the poet himself observed. And there were other demands that could not be evaded. In 1917 he was drafted for military service and, after officer's training at Parma, dispatched for active duty in the infantry at Vallarsa on the Trentino front. Of his military experience very little survives in his poetry except for the exquisite osso breve, "Valmorbia . . ." (see note thereon), and a late poem sardonically titled "L'eroismo" ("Heroism"),

---

[2] Ibid.

[3] In his account of his musical education, Montale allows the reader to understand that Sivori died in 1917, just as Montale was called into the army. In fact, the temporal closure was not so neat. See Giulio Nascimbeni, Montale: Biografia di un poeta (Milan, Loganesi & Co., 1986, 40).—R. W.

built around an incident in which Montale recognizes his own nature ("I didn't hate the enemy, and I couldn't have killed either man or beast"), and at the same time sees a "sign" of his vocation as a European, and not merely Italian, poet. On patrol one night, he had surprised three Austrian soldiers who had surrendered without a shot; in the pocket of one of his prisoners Montale discovered a copy of Rilke.

Demobilized in 1919, he returned to Genoa and the long summer vacations at Monterosso. Here he wrote poetry, read avidly and widely for six or seven hours daily, and formed part of the circle of regionalist and anti-D'Annunzian writers who gathered regularly at the Caffè Diana. It was poetry of the "proto-Montale," i.e., the poetry written after *"Meriggiare"* (1916) up to 1922, when his serious poetic work—the poems that compose the *Ossi*—clearly began. The poems that precede the *Ossi* consist of "Seacoasts" and a suite entitled *"Accordi: sensi e fantasmi di una adoloscente"* ("Chords: Sensations and Fancies of an Adolescent Girl"), each poem of which was devoted to the moody daydreamings of a young girl as she experiences various instruments of the orchestra. The impulse behind the suite would seem to have been not only Montale's youthful fascination with the impressionism of Debussy and "the naive pretense of imitating musical instruments," but a naive effort on the part of the aspirant singer to transfer musical impressions and ideas directly into poetic form. Montale himself was obviously embarrassed by them and was only reluctantly persuaded to republish them in 1962. And the only poems from the period 1916–1921 to make their way into *Ossi di seppia* are *"Meriggiare,"* "Seacoasts," and "English Horn" (see note thereon) from the *Accordi* suite.

A strenuous, lifelong reader, Montale was an autodidact of remarkable range and depth. Instead of enrolling in a university, he spent his days in the library of Genoa. Endowed with a musical ear, he quickly, and on his own, mastered French and Spanish and, to a lesser degree, English. In philosophy he was drawn, like almost all Italian intellectuals of the period, to the native Idealists, Benedetto Croce and Giovanni Gentile, and to Boutroux's philosophy of contingency as well as to Bergson. His preferred authors in English at this time were Shakespeare, Browning, and (I believe) Donne, as well as Henry James and, it seems, Gerard Manley Hopkins. But his essential intellectual orientation was toward the French writers, above all Baudelaire, Mallarmé, Guérin, Taine, Jammes, Lemaître, and Valéry. In Italian literature and thought he read the classic authors selectively but voraciously, as well as contemporary poets (e.g., D'Annunzio, Campana, etc.), dramatists (e.g., Pirandello, an oddly neglected "influence"), novelists, and critics. As Gianfranco Contini observed, Montale possessed that furious autodidactic energy not infrequently found among great thinkers and writers, for instance, Croce and Gide.

His daily reading done, Montale spent the evenings at the Caffé Diana. There he found good company: intellectuals and writers such as Angelo Barile, Adriano Grande (to whom the *Ossi* were dedicated), Pierangelo Baratono, and, most important, his friend, the gentle "crepuscular" regionalist, Camillo Sbarbaro. With the death of the critic and poet Giovanni Boine in 1917, and Ceccardo Roccatagliata Ceccardi in 1919, Sbarbaro had become the leading voice of Ligurian regionalism at the Diana. But despite Montale's admiration for Sbarbaro and his sympathy with the understated, anti-heroic, anti-D'Annunzian poetics of the "crepuscular" writers, Montale, always skeptical of dogmatic parochialisms, was never a convinced or practicing regionalist. His Liguria was, even more than Sbarbaro's, a real place, defined by exact particulars, precisely named and evoked. But, unlike Sbarbaro's and that of the other regionalists, it was also the poetic home of "a general truth." The distance between Montale and the regionalists of Caffé Diana can only be assessed by comparing their work, their poetics—Sbarbaro's, say—with the poems and poetics of *Ossi di seppia*.

In regard to D'Annunzio Montale's allusive discourse is more edged, less deferential. "For the rest of the nineteenth century after Leopardi," he wrote, "it was next to impossible to write poetry." Leopardi had simply exhausted the lyrical possibilities. And the same, he felt, was true of D'Annunzio, who "had experimented with and exploited all the linguistic and prosodic possibilities of our time." D'Annunzio was perceived as a "monstrous presence, something of whom had stuck to all poets who followed him." To English-speaking readers, unfamiliar with D'Annunzio's *oeuvre* and all too prone to dismiss him as a poet because of his Fascist affinities and vulgar heroics (known in Italy as *D'Annunzianismo*), it may come as a surprise that he could be perceived by Montale and others as the great literary lion-in-the-path. But we must, I believe, take Montale's word for the fact of D'Annunzio's prodigious poetic powers. He was a poet who, whatever we may think of the man, had brought the genius of the Italian language to what many thought was its lyrical fulfillment. The problem was, like that posed by Leopardi in the nineteenth century, how to write poetry after, and against, him. Guido Gozzano (1883–1916),[4] for instance, attempted to counter D'Annunzio's

---

[4] Gozzano provides the necessary step from the orotundity of Carducci and D'Annunzio's gorgeous rhetoric to elliptical, understated "Hermetic" poetry of the crepuscolari. Gozzano shares with the crepuscolari a "certain languor and a certain love of the faded." But his vigor, wit, and irony set him apart.

Born in Torino of a fairly affluent family, Gozzano published his first book, *La Via*

magnificent self-confidence with "crepuscular" irony, and self-deprecating humility. In Montale's opinion Gozzano had succeeded in evading his precursor's oppressiveness. Gozzano, he wrote, was a poet who knew his own limits. "A natural D'Annunzian, even more naturally disgusted by D'Annunzianism, he was the first twentieth-century poet to succeed in *traversing D'Annunzio* in order to make landfall in his own country, just as, on a larger scale, Baudelaire had traversed Hugo in order to lay the groundwork of a new poetry."

del rifugio *(The Road to Shelter),* in 1907; and in 1911 his *I Colloqui (Colloquys)* appeared and was enthusiastically hailed. He traveled to India and Ceylon in 1912. His work on a long book of poetic "entomological epistles" about butterflies *(Farfalle)* was never completed. He retired (or withdrew), and then died (of the tuberculosis that had plagued him for years) at Torino in August of 1916.

Gozzano's poetry is one of regret, sadness, nostalgia for *i bei tempi;* regret for lost or fleeting life, for unlived life above all. Gozzano speaks of himself as an exile, a voluntary exile, and a dreamer: "Let me dream" *("Ma lasciatemi sognare . . .").* The self-portrait of Gozzano that appears is that of a man prematurely old, weary of literary chitchat, but also loveless and unloving, indeed incapable of love; dried up, a cold man, a wintry mocker and sneerer, a seedless husk: *"ciarpame / reietto, cosi caro alla mia Musa."* Lover of small objects of no particular taste, of keepsakes, bric-a-brac, moldy or unfashionably out-of-date things. Above all is the constant lament for unlived life.

Montale on Gozzano:

> Why was Gozzano so immediately successful with *I Colloqui?* Because he was immediately read and understood by the readers of D'Annunzio and Pascoli and the minor D'Annunziani. He fitted into the public taste without arousing suspicion because he worked a sort of reduction upon the poetry that had preceded him. He presented a new species of poetry, the poetry of *faux-expres,* of semitones and harmonies in gray, the poetry not truly heroic, but *en pantoufles* that the French, Belgian, and Flemish post-symbolists had already been experimenting with for many years. . . . He stayed close to the verbal impasto of the *poema paradisiaco,* of the sounds and accents of D'Annunzio at his most crepuscular *(avant lettre).* . . .
>
> There was a verbal experiment in the air—plastic, lively, new— that had found in D'Annunzio its supreme craftsman, and that, stripped down, led D'Annunzio into the liveliest parts of his *Alcione.* Gozzano didn't push himself as far forward as *Alcione;* he stopped at the *Poema paradisiaco,* and he wrapped the bric-a-brac of the good things in terrible taste in a sumptuously *negligé* cloak. He was, verbally, a rich pauper, or a poor rich man. He reduced D'Annunzio as Debussy had reduced Wagner, but without ever arriving at results that we could call Debussy-like. . . . Gozzano reduced the Italian poetry of his time to its lowest common denominator. . . . [*"Gozzano, dopo trent'anni," Lo Smeraldo,* vol. V, no. 5 (30 September 1951), 3–8; reprinted as introduction to Gozzano's *Poesie* (Milan, 1960) and in *Sulla Poesia* (Milan, 1976), 54–62.]

Influence

Montale's relation to Italian literary tradition is far too complex for present discussion, but too important to be scanted altogether. In any case the definitive account of the influence of earlier Italian poets, above all the undeniably crucial influence of Dante, Leopardi, and D'Annunzio, has yet to be written, though perceptive studies of individual influence by all three exist. What is urgently needed is not further documentation of echoes but discussion of the mode and rationale of Montale's allusive practice generally. It is my conviction that Montale's allusions are almost never decorative or traditional embellishments of theme or situation, *but are rather structural elements* designed to suggest or establish a deeper point of view, an attitude or stance essential to, but incapable of being directly stated by, the poem.[5] The poet appeals to a strong voice of his own tradition, not in order to enlist its authority in the service of his poem, but rather to enter into dialogue with it in order to clarify or qualify his individual differences. Like Eliot's "individual talent," the poet's voice becomes a dialectical modification of the tradition, a voice that in turn, if it succeeds, modifies the tradition it continues.

For Montale as for Eliot, the point was programmatic. Thus in his 1925 essay, "Style and Tradition," Montale expressed the hope that his work "might contribute to the development of a cordial atmosphere of allusion and understanding in which an artistic expression, however modest, might emerge without being misinterpreted." The result would be a welcome climate of what he termed "superior dilettantism." By this he meant, of course, not as it might seem to us, highbrow superficiality but rather a lofty, knowingly mediated and humanly discerning engagement with tradition, an attitude utterly distinct from the Fascists' shoddy pretense of renewing a past greatness of which they had no understanding whatever. Nothing of course could come of abject deference toward tradition, as evidenced by Italian literary mandarinism, with its exaltation of the aulic and its contempt for the colloquial as well as that *vita vissuta*—that *lived life* whose natural language is the *spoken* language, the *parlato*. What mattered to Montale was that living men should not do violence to their own memories by declaring, like the Futurists, that the

---

[5] In the case of Dante, see Glauco Cambon's *Eugenio Montale's Poetry: A Dream in Reason's Presence* (Princeton, 1982) and Arshi Pipa's *Montale and Dante* (Minneapolis, 1968). On Leopardi, see Gilberto Lonardi's *"Lungo l'asse leopardiano"* in *Il vecchio e il giovane e altri studi su Montale* (Bologna, 1980) and the exceptionally illuminating essay by Claire de C. L. Huffman, "Eugenio Montale and Giacomo Leopardi," *Italian Quarterly,* xxviii (Summer / Fall 1987), 25–34. On D'Annunzio see Pier Vincenzo Mengaldo, *La traduzione del novecento* (Milan, 1972) and Joseph Cary, *Three Modern Italian Poets: Saba, Ungaretti, Montale* (New York, 1969; 2d edition, revised and enlarged, Chicago, 1993), 254.

past has been superseded; or like the Fascists, that the past was Fascist too; or by the mandarin *littérateurs,* that the past they had embalmed should mortify the living. Without memory, the individual had no identity; without memory of its civilized past, its traditions and values, a society deprived itself of a manworthy[6] future.

In the *Ossi,* for instance, Montale repeatedly (and rather more frequently than critics have allowed) alludes to Dante. Thus, the blazing, blinding light of the Mediterranean noon is persistently evoked; but it is almost as often, as in *"Don't take shelter . . ."* and *"Bring me the sunflower . . . ,"* invested with the metaphysical or transcendental light—Dante's *luce intellettuale.* The investment is designed not to sound a consonantly Dantesque note, but rather to indicate a crucial degree of difference *from* Dante, established by context and subtly developed dissonance of attitude and belief. Montale invokes Dante because they share a fundamental (idealistic / poetic) kinship, but also because Montale's strong belief in immanence divides him from Dante's transcendental theology. "The transcendental 'I,' " wrote Montale, "is a light that . . . carries us toward a nonindividual, and therefore nonhuman condition." There is an abyss below but also above. For Montale, the human condition lies between, defined by a body weighed down by animal gravity and therefore, dialectically on fire with "immortal leanings," disposed to the divine, which it intermittently reveals. And even in other passages clearly evocative of Dante, above all in the "Noons and Shadows" section of the *Ossi,* but also, in *"To laze at noon . . . ,"* the allusive purpose is to identify a Dantesque situation but at the same time to attach it to a different context, an experience of hell, both old and new, that makes of it a fresh variant on the great traditional tale of human destiny. Montale's version does not merely repeat Dante's, but harmoniously, cordially, amends it.

Montale's allusions to Leopardi perpend, many of them, the same dialectical engagement.

About the *Ossi di seppia*

An astute and scrupulously honest self-critic, Montale gave a characteristically spare account of the making of his first book. *Cuttlefish Bones,* he observed in his "Imaginary Interview" written some twenty years later, was a book "that wrote itself." By this he meant that the book was devoid of philosophical and programmatic intentions. He had, he explained, simply "obeyed a need for musical expression." Given the poems themselves and the voluminous, often philosophical commentary

---

[6][W. A. cherished the epithet "manworthy" for its resonances from Coleridge and Emerson (see *O.E.D.* 'man" 19d), and he insisted on the continuing life of the word.—*R. W.*]

they have evoked,[7] this might seem a disarming effort at poetic modesty. But this is to misunderstand Montale's mind, instinctively, unconsciously philosophical and, like the Italian mind generally in the first half of the century, suffused, often unawares, with Crocean idealism, saturated in its categories of thought. Montale's "need for musical expression" was shaped by a point of view manifestly, though perhaps naively, philosophical. The evidence is in the poems themselves, but also in Montale's own later account:

> I obeyed a need for musical expression. I wanted my words to come closer than those of other poets I had read. Closer to what? I seemed to be living under a bell jar, and yet I felt I was close to something essential. A delicate veil, a thread, barely separated me from that definitive *quid*. Absolute expression would have meant breaking that veil, that thread: an explosion, the end of the illusion of the world as representation. But this remained an unattainable goal. And my desire to come close remained musical, instinctive, unprogrammatic. I wanted to wring the neck of the eloquence of our old aulic language, even at the risk of a countereloquence.[8]

If the early Montale was unconscious of the purposiveness, both philosophical and programmatic, in his "need for musical expression," the later Montale acknowledges in it the allusions here to Schopenhauer, Rimbaud, and Verlaine.

[From this point onward, the introduction is composed of notes left by W. A.]

"I wrote the book with clenched teeth," Montale proceeds—a statement that at first sight seems a denial of a book that "wrote itself." But the contradiction is merely apparent. What tormented Montale in writing the *Ossi* was precisely that "musical expression": the anguish of acquiring a true individual voice, of mastering tone, nuance, and timbre through difficult, patiently disciplined trial and error. What had to be avoided was above all the old Mandarin poetic rhetoric, the Italian curse of easy virtuosity, of aulic inflation, facile *solfeggio*, all-too-predictable cadences. In his dislike of such literary inflation, rhetorical embellishment, and poetic posturing, his own "anti-D'Annunzian" poetics became

---

[7] See, for instance, Calvino's commentary on "Maybe one morning . . . ," quoted on p. 214 of the Notes to the translation.

[8] *"Intenzioni (Intervista immaginaria),"* Op. cit.

a *deliberate impoverishment* of poetic means—a tough, harsh tenacity in staying with hard things, hard sounds, hard words.

It is important to emphasize that the *Ossi* is not, as early Italian critics of it too readily assumed, regional poetry in the vein of Ceccardi, Boine, and Sbarbaro. For Solmi what makes Montale's poetry "classical" is its aspiration to move beyond the landscape: in sum, its idealism.[9] For Montale the aspiration toward transcendence seems, in the poet's case, to be, despite occasional outbursts, embodied by others. But if the ability to transcend is *vicarious,* the passion is Montalean. Thus Solmi observes, about "House by the Sea," that the poem adumbrates a theme dear to Montale, "the sense of a failed and enclosed life, despairing now of being equal to its original idea, which subsides in a tired sacrifice in order that others, the beloved creature, escape from 'the limbo of maimed existences,' succeed in living fully and saving itself."[10]

A way out of the "blockaded self"? In this connection one must bear in mind what Montale said of Svevo, who had "in three successive self-portraits created the myth of himself, and I would almost say the category of a *senilità* that is not temporal but is the state-of-being of whoever feels he has already lived for himself and others, suffered and lived for all."[11] This is *senilità* as a *vocation.* Yet Montale quietly rejects any statement or hint that might announce the unity of a self. The dominant voice of the *Ossi* is one that is trying to locate, to express, its own still emerging certitudes. The multiplicity is daunting, as is the evanescence of postures, positions, attitudes. No sooner does the poet begin to sound a confident note than he rejects it. The voice is tentative, the verse full of detours and deliberate indirections. Civic, social, and political concerns seem lacking. But a social world survives in a penumbra around the poems.

Montale in the *Ossi* also evinces a constant misgiving about knowledge; he seems to gird himself against conclusions that might be premature or false, in danger of foreclosing more spacious possibilities of meaning and becoming. About transcendence he is always ambivalent. There is admiration in his line from "House by the Sea" that "transcendence may perhaps be theirs who want it," but also mordant irony. The *nisus* per-

---

[9] Cf. Croce or, in a similar vein, Bradley: "Finite existence and perfection are incompatible. . . . The ideal and the real can never be at one. But their division is precisely what we mean by imperfection. And thus incompleteness, and unrest, and unsatisfied ideality, are the lot of the finite." Bradley, *Appearance and Reality* (2nd ed., Oxford, 1897), 217.

[10] Cf. "House by the Sea," p. 151.

[11] Eugenio Montale and Italo Svevo, *Lettere (con gli scritti di Montale su Svevo)* (Bari, De Donato, 1966), 154. [Pages 149–76 print the famous lecture on Svevo by Montale, entitled *"Italo Svevo nel Centennario della nascita,"* delivered in Trieste in 1963 at the *Circolo della Cultura e delle Arti.*—C. H.]

sists, however, as it does not in, say, the accomplished diffidence of Ashbery's poetry. Montale's taste for ending poems in an aposiopesis (see "Slope," p. 131) is based on a suspicious dislike of concludings as violations of process or of thought itself: there is always something else, something more, to be said. *Tertium quid datur.* The poems exhibit a purposive indirection, becoming more pronounced, less umbratile, in the final sequence of the book. The motions of his mind are serpentine, designed to render the intricate shifts, loopings, detours, and contradictions inherent in self-making.

At the same time the poems, and the poet, seem to be in search of identity, and therefore in search of liberating examples—liberation too of *self* in recognition and discovery of *others*. The unity of the *Ossi* is that of an evolving, emerging life paratactically revealed in its successive stages like the hatching of a larva from its egg: the poetics of eclosion, a daimonic process, life as a constant *fluire* registered in the unfolding of the poems. The book engages what Joseph Cary has aptly termed "the diaristic or fragmented mode." This slowly evolving life has its stages, but also its rhythms of both advance and regression, its diapauses and progress, on the way to eclosion. It reveals Montale as poetic entomologist, the entomologist already visible even in the poems preceding "Chrysalis."

Italo Calvino speaks of Montale's thematic insistence that, if there is any hope in his thought, it must connect with the ability to pass through the wasteland.

> . . . this difficult heroism dug in one's very gut, and in the aridity and precariousness of existence, this anti-heroic heroism, is that answer that Montale gave to the problems of poetry in his generation: how to write verse after (and against) D'Annunzio (and after Carducci, and after Pascoli, or at least a certain image of Pascoli). . . . There is no message of consolation or encouragement in Montale unless we accept the awareness of an inhospitable and stinting universe. It is along this arduous path that his message continues that of Leopardi, even if their voices sound very different. In the same way, Montale's atheism is more problematical than Leopardi's, shot through with continual leaning toward something supernatural that is at once corroded by his basic skepticism. . . .[12]

Montale's *inetto,* or "prematurely old" protagonist, is really the condition of modern man, not merely a self-portrait of fecklessly private

[12] Italo Calvino, *The Uses of Literature,* tr. Patrick Creagh (San Diego, 1986), 288.

ineptitude (the type in Gozzano, Svevo, and Tozzi). In Montale's critical prose he remarked that the result of this new human condition was "a new modern man," the antihero. And this new condition called for new poetic means, a poetics of self-extinction, *dépouillement,* and impoverishment of inherited rhetoric, a process begun in *Ossi di seppia* that would lead uncompromisingly into the harsh prosaic work of the final volumes.

Acknowledgments

In translating these poems I have been blessed in obtaining tough, astute, and generous help from friends, colleagues, and Montaleani, both professional and amateur. To Gertrude Hooker I owe quite a special burden of thanks for her bracing and discerning critiques of each and every poem, in numerous versions. Even when I disagreed with her, the need to articulate those differences proved instructive, forcing me to clarify and justify whatever principles of translation guided my poetic hunches and practice. I am also deeply grateful for the painstaking criticism provided by D. S. Carne-Ross, Joseph Cary, Simone Di Piero, Claire Huffman, W. S. Merwin, Massimo Piatelli-Palmarini, and Rosanna Warren. For whatever errors remain I am solely responsible.

In limine

Godi se il vento ch'entra nel pomario
vi rimena l'ondata della vita:
qui dove affonda un morto
viluppo di memorie,
orto non era, ma reliquiario.

Il frullo che tu senti non è un volo,
ma il commuoversi dell'eterno grembo;
vedi che si trasforma questo lembo
di terra solitario in un crogiuolo.

Un rovello è di qua dall'erto muro.
Se procedi t'imbatti
tu forse nel fantasma che ti salva:
si compongono qui le storie, gli atti
scancellati pel giuoco del futuro.

Cerca una maglia rotta nella rete
che ci stringe, tu balza fuori, fuggi!
Va, per te l'ho pregato,—ora la sete
mi sarà lieve, meno acre la ruggine . . .

Rejoice when the breeze that enters the orchard
brings you back the tidal rush of life:
here, where dead memories
mesh and founder,
was no garden, but a reliquary.

That surge you hear is no whir of wings,
but the stirring of the eternal womb.
Look how this strip of lonely coast
has been transformed: a crucible.

All is furor within the sheer wall.
Advance, and you may chance upon
the phantasm who might save you:
here are tales composed and deeds
annulled, for the future to enact.

Find a break in the meshes of the net
that tightens around us, leap out, flee!
Go, I have prayed for your escape—now my thirst
will be slaked, my rancor less bitter . . .

Movements

I limoni

Ascoltami, i poeti laureati
si muovono soltanto fra le piante
dai nomi poco usati: bossi ligustri o acanti.
Io, per me, amo le strade che riescono agli erbosi
fossi dove in pozzanghere
mezzo seccate agguantano i ragazzi
qualche sparuta anguilla:
le viuzze che seguono i ciglioni,
discendono tra i ciuffi delle canne
e mettono negli orti, tra gli alberi dei limoni.

Meglio se le gazzarre degli uccelli
si spengono inghiottite dall'azzurro:
più chiaro si ascolta il susurro
dei rami amici nell'aria che quasi non si muove,
e i sensi di quest'odore
che non sa staccarsi da terra
e piove in petto una dolcezza inquieta.
Qui delle divertite passioni
per miracolo tace la guerra,
qui tocca anche a noi poveri la nostra parte di ricchezza
ed è l'odore dei limoni.

Vedi, in questi silenzi in cui le cose
s'abbandonano e sembrano vicine
a tradire il loro ultimo segreto,
talora ci si aspetta
di scoprire uno sbaglio di Natura,
il punto morto del mondo, l'anello che non tiene,
il filo da disbrogliare che finalmente ci metta
nel mezzo di una verità.
Lo sguardo fruga d'intorno,
la mente indaga accorda disunisce

The Lemon Trees

Listen: the laureled poets
stroll only among shrubs
with learned names: ligustrum, acanthus, box.
What I like are streets that end in grassy
ditches where boys snatch
a few famished eels from drying puddles:
paths that struggle along the banks,
then dip among the tufted canes,
into the orchards, among the lemon trees.

Better, if the gay palaver of the birds
is stilled, swallowed by the blue:
more clearly now, you hear the whisper
of genial branches in that air barely astir,
the sense of that smell
inseparable from earth,
that rains its restless sweetness in the heart.
Here, by some miracle, the war
of conflicted passions is stilled,
here even we the poor share the riches of the world—
the smell of the lemon trees.

See, in these silences when things
let themselves go and seem almost
to reveal their final secret,
we sometimes expect
to discover a flaw in Nature,
the world's dead point, the link that doesn't hold,
the thread that, disentangled, might at last lead us
to the center of a truth.
The eye rummages,
the mind pokes about, unifies, disjoins
in the fragrance that grows

nel profumo che dilaga
quando il giorno più languisce.
Sono i silenzi in cui si vede
in ogni ombra umana che si allontana
qualche disturbata Divinità.

Ma l'illusione manca e ci riporta il tempo
nelle città rumorose dove l'azzurro si mostra
soltanto a pezzi, in alto, tra le cimase.
La pioggia stanca la terra, di poi; s'affolta
il tedio dell'inverno sulle case,
la luce si fa avara—amara l'anima.
Quando un giorno da un malchiuso portone
tra gli alberi di una corte
ci si mostrano i gialli dei limoni;
e il gelo del cuore si sfa,
e in petto ci scrosciano
le loro canzoni
le trombe d'oro della solarità.

as the day closes, languishing.
These are the silences where we see
in each departing human shade
some disturbed Divinity.

But the illusion dies, time returns us
to noisy cities where the sky is only
patches of blue, high up, between the cornices.
Rain wearies the ground; over the buildings
winter's tedium thickens.
Light grows niggardly, the soul bitter.
And, one day, through a gate ajar,
among the trees in a courtyard,
we see the yellows of the lemon trees;
and the heart's ice thaws,
and songs pelt
into the breast
and trumpets of gold pour forth
epiphanies of Light!

Corno inglese

Il vento che stasera suona attento
—ricorda un forte scotere di lame—
gli strumenti dei fitti alberi e spazza
l'orizzonte di rame
dove strisce di luce si protendono
come aquiloni al cielo che rimbomba
(Nuvole in viaggio, chiari
reami di lassù! D'alti Eldoradi
malchiuse porte!)
e il mare che scaglia a scaglia,
livido, muta colore,
lancia a terra una tromba
di schiume intorte;
il vento che nasce e muore
nell'ora che lenta s'annera
suonasse te pure stasera
scordato strumento,
cuore.

English Horn

Tonight this wind intently playing
(a wild clangor of blades comes to mind)
instruments of serried trees, that sweep
the copper horizon
where stripes of light reach up
like kites, and the sky rings the clamor back
(Clouds in transit, shining kingdoms
aloft! High Eldorados,
portals ajar!),
and the sea, scale upon scale,
ashen, changes color,
and hurls to earth a trumpet spout
of twisted spume;
this wind that lifts and dies
in the slowly darkening hour—
if only it could play on you
this night, O discordant
heart!

Falsetto

Esterina, i vent'anni ti minacciano,
grigiorosea nube
che a poco a poco in sé ti chiude.
Ciò intendi e non paventi.
Sommersa ti vedremo
nella fumea che il vento
lacera o addensa, violento.
Poi dal fiotto di cenere uscirai
adusta più che mai,
proteso a un'avventura più lontana
l'intento viso che assembra
l'arciera Diana.
Salgono i venti autunni,
t'avviluppano andate primavere;
ecco per te rintocca
un presagio nell'elisie sfere.
Un suono non ti renda
qual d'incrinata brocca
percossa!; io prego sia
per te concerto ineffabile
di sonagliere.

La dubbia dimane non t'impaura.
Leggiadra ti distendi
sullo scoglio lucente di sale
e al sole bruci le membra.
Ricordi la lucertola
ferma sul masso brullo;
te insidia giovinezza,
quella il lacciòlo d'erba del fanciullo.
L'acqua è la forza che ti tempra,
nell'acqua ti ritrovi e ti rinnovi:
noi ti pensiamo come un'alga, un ciottolo,

Falsetto

Esterina, your twentieth year now threatens,
a cloud of grayish pink
that day by day enswathes you.
You know, and you're not afraid.
We'll see you in the waves, swallowed
by smoky haze torn
or thickened by the raging wind.
Later you'll rise from ashen breakers,
more sunburnt than ever,
stretching toward some new adventure,
your face so intense you might be
the huntress Diana.
Your twenty autumns mount,
springtimes past enfold you;
and now for you a presage rings
in Elysian spheres.
May it never be a cracked urn struck
you hear; my prayer for you
is a peal of bells
ineffable.

Anxious tomorrows leave you unafraid.
All grace, you stretch
on the rock ledge shining with salt
and burn your body in the sun.
I think of a lizard
stock-still on the bare rock.
Youth lies in wait for you, like a boy's
grass noose waiting for the lizard.
The power that tempers you is water,
in water you find and renew yourself.
I think of you as seaweed, a pebble,
an ocean creature

come un'equorea creatura
che la salsedine non intacca
ma torna al lito più pura.

Hai ben ragione tu! Non turbare
di ubbie il sorridente presente.
La tua gaiezza impegna già il futuro
ed un crollar di spalle
dirocca i fortilizî
del tuo domani oscuro.
T'alzi e t'avanzi sul ponticello
esiguo, sopra il gorgo che stride:
il tuo profilo s'incide
contro uno sfondo di perla.
Esiti a sommo del tremulo asse,
poi ridi, e come spiccata da un vento
t'abbatti fra le braccia
del tuo divino amico che t'afferra.

Ti guardiamo noi, della razza
di chi rimane a terra.

uncorrupted by salt,
homing to the beach, purer than before.

How right you are! This happy moment
is yours! Live now, unafraid!
Already your gaiety engages the future;
a shrug of your shoulders
topples the bastion
of your unknown tomorrow.
You rise, step out on that small
thin plank above the screeching abyss,
profile incised
against a background of pearl.
At the tip of the trembling board you hesitate,
laugh, and then, as though ravished by a wind,
plunge to the welcoming arms
of your divine lover.

We watch you—we, of the race of those
who cling to the shore.

Minstrels

da C. Debussy

Ritornello, rimbalzi
tra le vetrate d'afa dell'estate.

Acre groppo di note soffocate,
riso che non esplode
ma trapunge le ore vuote
e lo suonano tre avanzi di baccanale
vestiti di ritagli di giornali,
con istrumenti mai veduti,
simili a strani imbuti
che si gonfiano a volte e poi s'afflosciano.

Musica senza rumore
che nasce dalle strade,
s'innalza a stento e ricade,
e si colora di tinte
ora scarlatte ora biade,
e inumidisce gli occhi, così che il mondo
si vede come socchiudendo gli occhi
nuotar nel biondo.

Scatta ripiomba sfuma,
poi riappare
soffocata e lontana: si consuma.
Non s'ode quasi, si respira.
                              Bruci
tu pure tra le lastre dell'estate,
cuore che ti smarrisci! Ed ora incauto
provi le ignote note sul tuo flauto.

Minstrels

after Debussy

Refrain rebounding
from panes of muggy summer heat:

acrid knot of suffocated notes,
baffled laughter that strains to break free,
stabbing through empty hours,
and three remnants from some Bacchanalian rout
draped in newspaper clippings
with instruments no man has ever seen,
weird funnels that sporadically
bulge, then collapse.

Soundless music
lifting from the streets
struggles to climb, falls back,
takes on color,
now scarlet, now bright blue,
so moistening the eyes it seems
the lids are closed, the world
aswim with gold.

Leaps, plunges, fades,
then resumes,
strangled, remote: consumed.
Almost unheard, a breath.
                          You burn too,
faint heart, baffled between the summer's
windowpanes! And now, impulsive,
your flute fumbles the unknown notes.

POESIE PER CAMILLO SBARBARO

I

Caffè a Rapallo

Natale nel tepidario
lustrante, truccato dai fumi
che svolgono tazze, velato
tremore di lumi oltre i chiusi
cristalli, profili di femmine
nel grigio, tra lampi di gemme
e screzi di sete . . .
               Son giunte
a queste native tue spiagge,
le nuove Sirene!; e qui manchi
Camillo, amico, tu storico
di cupidige e di brividi.

S'ode grande frastuono nella via.

È passata di fuori
l'indicibile musica
delle trombe di lama
e dei piattini arguti dei fanciulli:
è passata la musica innocente.

Un mondo gnomo ne andava
con strepere di muletti e di carriole,
tra un lagno di montoni
di cartapesta e un bagliare
di sciabole fasciate di stagnole.
Passarono i Generali
con le feluche di cartone

POEMS FOR CAMILLO SBARBARO

I

Café at Rapallo

Christmas in the gleaming
tepidarium, cosmetic
fumes coiling from cups, curtained
shimmer of lights from beyond closed
panes, women profiled
in soft light among blazing jewels
and shot silk. . . .
     They've arrived,
the new Sirens, on your native
shores! And now we need you, here,
old friend, Camillo, chronicler
of thrills and desires.

From the street a wild racket.

Outside the café
an indescribable music paraded by—
a blare of tin bugles, a silvery
tinkle of children's baptismal saucers:
the music of innocence passed us by.

With it marched a goblin world
in a clatter of tiny donkeys and carts,
and a bleat of *papier-mâché*
rams, and a gleam
of sabers sheathed in foil.
The generals, cocked hats
of cardboard, brandishing nougat

e impugnavano aste di torroni;
poi furono i gregari
con moccoli e lampioni,
e le tinnanti scatole
ch'ànno il suono più trito,
tenue rivo che incanta
l'animo dubitoso:
(meraviglioso udivo).

L'orda passò col rumore
d'una zampante greggia
che il tuono recente impaura.
L'accolse la pastura
che per noi più non verdeggia.

lances, passed by;
and then the rank and file
with candles and lanterns,
and little boxes
that rattled with the tinniest sounds,
a stream of children to enthrall
the skeptical soul:
(I listened and marveled).

The horde passed with the roar
of a frightened herd stampeding
from a sudden burst of thunder.
It found shelter in that greening pasture
where you and I will never graze again.

2

Epigramma

Sbarbaro, estroso fanciullo, piega versicolori
carte e ne trae navicelle che affida alla fanghiglia
mobile d'un rigagno; vedile andarsene fuori.
Sii preveggente per lui, tu galantuomo che passi:
col tuo bastone raggiungi la delicata flottiglia,
che non si perda; guidala a un porticello di sassi.

2

Epigram

Sbarbaro, whimsical lad, maker of varicolored
paper boats, launches them in the flowing mud
of the gutter: look at them sail away!
Kind sir, take forethought for the boy:
hook that flotilla with your cane
before it founders; nudge it to its cove of pebbles.

Quasi una fantasia

Raggiorna, lo presento
da un albore di frusto
argento alle pareti:
lista un barlume le finestre chiuse.
Torna l'avvenimento
del sole e le diffuse
voci, i consueti strepiti non porta.

Perché? Penso ad un giorno d'incantesimo
e delle giostre d'ore troppo uguali
mi ripago. Traboccherà la forza
che mi turgeva, incosciente mago,
da grande tempo. Ora m'affaccerò,
subisserò alte case, spogli viali.

Avrò di contro un paese d'intatte nevi
ma lievi come viste in un arazzo.
Scivolerà dal cielo bioccoso un tardo raggio.
Gremite d'invisibile luce selve e colline
mi diranno l'elogio degl'ilari ritorni.

Lieto leggerò i neri
segni dei rami sul bianco
come un essenziale alfabeto.
Tutto il passato in un punto
dinanzi mi sarà comparso.
Non turberà suono alcuno
quest'allegrezza solitaria.
Filerà nell'aria
o scenderà s'un paletto
qualche galletto di marzo.

Almost a Fantasia

Daylight again, I sense it
in the dawning of old
silver on the walls:
a glimmer edges the shut windows.
The sun comes back
again, but brings
no diffused voices, no customary din.

Why? I think of a day of enchantment,
my reward for the pageant of hours
too much alike. In me the power
welling, unconscious wizard,
will overflow. Yes, I'll be standing at the window,
I'll overwhelm tall houses, treeless streets.

Before me will be a land of virgin snow,
but powdered, as in a tapestry.
From a fleecy sky a slow radiance will slide.
Flooded with invisible light, forests and hills
will sing in praise of joyous returnings.

Elated, I'll read the black
signs of branches on the white,
like an alphabet of being.
In an instant, and the whole past
will open out before me.
No sound will jar
this solitary joy.
Easing through the air
or gliding to a perch,
a hoopoe or two will come
to usher in the spring.

SARCOFAGHI

Dove se ne vanno le ricciute donzelle
che recano le colme anfore su le spalle
ed hanno il fermo passo sì leggero;
e in fondo uno sbocco di valle
invano attende le belle
cui adombra una pergola di vigna
e i grappoli ne pendono oscillando.
Il sole che va in alto,
le intraviste pendici
non han tinte: nel blando
minuto la natura fulminata
atteggia le felici
sue creature, madre non matrigna,
in levità di forme.
Mondo che dorme o mondo che si gloria
d'immutata esistenza, chi può dire?,
uomo che passi, e tu dagli
il meglio ramicello del tuo orto.
Poi segui: in questa valle
non è vicenda di buio e di luce.
Lungi di qui la tua via ti conduce,
non c'è asilo per te, sei troppo morto:
seguita il giro delle tue stelle.
E dunque addio, infanti ricciutelle,
portate le colme anfore su le spalle.

SARCOPHAGI

where girls with wavy hair pass by,
jars of wine brimming on their shoulders,
firm of foot, stepping softly;
and down below a valley opens out,
waiting in vain for the lovely girls
shaded by a trellis of vines
heavy with swaying clusters.
The sun that mounts the sky,
the half-seen slopes, all
are colorless: in this mild
moment, Nature, in a lightning flash—
mother, no stepmother—
poses her creatures
in such grace of form.
World asleep or world that boasts
life unchanging, who can say?
O passerby, grace it,
give it your garden's loveliest bough.
Then go your way: this valley knows
no alternation of dark and light.
Your journey takes you far from here.
No refuge here for one so dead as you:
go, follow the orbit of your stars.
And so farewell, girls with wavy hair,
jars of wine brimming on your shoulders.

Ora sia il tuo passo
più cauto: a un tiro di sasso
di qui ti si prepara
una più rara scena.
La porta corrosa d'un tempietto
è rinchiusa per sempre.
Una grande luce è diffusa
sull'erbosa soglia.
E qui dove peste umane
non suoneranno, o fittizia doglia,
vigila steso al suolo un magro cane.
Mai più si muoverà
in quest'ora che s'indovina afosa.
Sopra il tetto s'affaccia
una nuvola grandiosa.

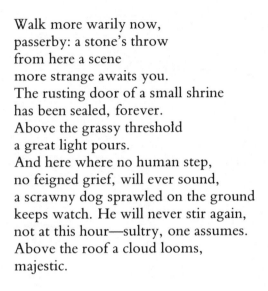

Walk more warily now,
passerby: a stone's throw
from here a scene
more strange awaits you.
The rusting door of a small shrine
has been sealed, forever.
Above the grassy threshold
a great light pours.
And here where no human step,
no feigned grief, will ever sound,
a scrawny dog sprawled on the ground
keeps watch. He will never stir again,
not at this hour—sultry, one assumes.
Above the roof a cloud looms,
majestic.

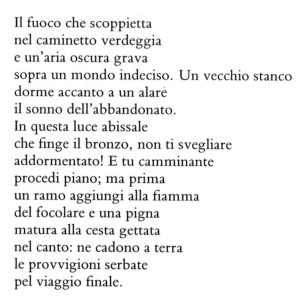

Il fuoco che scoppietta
nel caminetto verdeggia
e un'aria oscura grava
sopra un mondo indeciso. Un vecchio stanco
dorme accanto a un alare
il sonno dell'abbandonato.
In questa luce abissale
che finge il bronzo, non ti svegliare
addormentato! E tu camminante
procedi piano; ma prima
un ramo aggiungi alla fiamma
del focolare e una pigna
matura alla cesta gettata
nel canto: ne cadono a terra
le provvigioni serbate
pel viaggio finale.

The fire crackling
on the hearth flares green,
the dusky air presses down
on a world undecided. Beside the andiron
an old man sleeps the dead
sleep of the derelict.
In this abysmal light limned
in bronze, may you never waken
from your sleep! And you, passerby,
walk softly; but before you leave,
add your branch to the fire
blazing on the hearth, place
one ripe pinecone in that hamper chiseled
at the corner—out of which
provisions packed for the last journey spill
to the ground.

Ma dove cercare la tomba
dell'amico fedele e dell'amante;
quella del mendicante e del fanciullo;
dove trovare un asilo
per codesti che accolgono la brace
dell'originale fiammata;
oh da un segnale di pace lieve come un trastullo
l'urna ne sia effigiata!
Lascia la taciturna folla di pietra
per le derelitte lastre
ch'ànno talora inciso
il simbolo che più turba
poiché il pianto ed il riso
parimenti ne sgorgano, gemelli.
Lo guarda il triste artiere che al lavoro si reca
e già gli batte ai polsi una volontà cieca.
Tra quelle cerca un fregio primordiale
che sappia pel ricordo che ne avanza
trarre l'anima rude
per vie di dolci esigli:
un nulla, un girasole che si schiude
ed intorno una danza di conigli . . .

But where is the lover's tomb
and the faithful friend's;
the beggar's grave, the little boy's;
where do they repose,
those who welcome the embers
of the original flame?
Oh, carve their urns with some sign of peace
light as a toy!
Turn from the speechless crowd of stone
toward the abandoned slabs
here and there incised
with the symbol that most disturbs
since in it grief and laughter
are equal, twinned.
The sculptor, sadly gazing, goes back to work,
a blind will throbbing at his pulse,
searching among the slabs for a frieze so primal
it knows, remembering, what entices
the rough soul
on its road to gracious exile—
some trifle, a sunflower unfolding
and rabbits dancing around it. . . .

ALTRI VERSI

Vento e bandiere

La folata che alzò l'amaro aroma
del mare alle spirali delle valli,
e t'investì, ti scompigliò la chioma,
groviglio breve contro il cielo pallido;

la raffica che t'incollò la veste
e ti modulò rapida a sua imagine,
com'è tornata, te lontana, a queste
pietre che sporge il monte alla voragine;

e come spenta la furia briaca
ritrova ora il giardino il sommesso alito
che ti cullò, riversa sull'amaca,
tra gli alberi, ne' tuoi voli senz'ali.

Ahimè, non mai due volte configura
il tempo in egual modo i grani! E scampo
n'è: ché, se accada, insieme alla natura
la nostra fiaba brucerà in un lampo.

Sgorgo che non s'addoppia,—ed or fa vivo
un gruppo di abitati che distesi
allo sguardo sul fianco d'un declivo
si parano di gale e di palvesi.

Il mondo esiste . . . Uno stupore arresta
il cuore che ai vaganti incubi cede,
messaggeri del vespero: e non crede
che gli uomini affamati hanno una festa.

OTHER VERSES

Wind and Banners

The gust that lofted the brackish saltwater
smell to the looping valleys;
that assailed you, tousling your hair,
an instant's tangle against the pale sky;

the squall that wrapped you in your dress,
molding your body to its likeness—
and that now, unlike you, returns
to these cliffs fronting the sea's fury;

and how, that drunken rage once spent,
the garden finds again the gentle breeze
that lulled your wingless flights
in the hammock there between the trees.

Ah, but time never shapes its sands
the same way twice. And this sets us free:
otherwise our tale and Nature's too
would vanish in a flash.

Uprush never to be repeated—and now
a cluster of villages springs to view,
staggered along a hillside, each
festooned with bunting and banners.

The world *is*. . . . The heart, prey
to roving nightmares, messengers of evening,
stops in disbelief, amazed
that starving men should keep such holiday.

Fuscello teso dal muro . . .

Fuscello teso dal muro
sì come l'indice d'una
meridiana che scande la carriera
del sole e la mia, breve;
in una additi i crepuscoli
e alleghi sul tonaco
che imbeve la luce d'accesi
riflessi—e t'attedia la ruota
che in ombra sul piano dispieghi,
t'è noja infinita la volta
che stacca da te una smarrita
sembianza come di fumo
e grava con l'infittita
sua cupola mai dissolta.

Ma tu non adombri stamane
più il tuo sostegno ed un velo
che nella notte hai strappato
a un'orda invisibile pende
dalla tua cima e risplende
ai primi raggi. Laggiù,
dove la piana si scopre
del mare, un trealberi carico
di ciurma e di preda reclina
il bordo a uno spiro, e via scivola.
Chi è in alto e s'affaccia s'avvede
che brilla la tolda e il timone
nell'acqua non scava una traccia.

Shoot stretching from the wall . . .

Shoot stretching from the wall
so like the pointer on the dial
that tracks the sun's course
and my brief transit too:
While you mark the coming on of dusk,
your roots dig into plaster
soaked with the late light's ruddy
reflections—and the wheel your shadow
makes on the dial's face
wears you out, and your boredom
is boundless beneath that vault
of sky that severs from you
a stray, smokelike double
that presses down with its dense
indissoluble dome.

But this morning your shadow no longer falls
on the supporting wall, and a gauze
you plucked at night
from an unseen horde
dangles from your tip and shimmers
in the dawn light. Far below,
in the wide expanse of sea, a trawler,
three-masted, heaves into view,
ballasted with crew and catch,
heels with the wind and sheers away.
A man watching from the lookout sees
the deck that shines, and a rudder
that cuts the water and leaves no trace.

Cuttlefish Bones

Non chiederci la parola che squadri da ogni lato
l'animo nostro informe, e a lettere di fuoco
lo dichiari e risplenda come un croco
perduto in mezzo a un polveroso prato.

Ah l'uomo che se ne va sicuro,
agli altri ed a se stesso amico,
e l'ombra sua non cura che la canicola
stampa sopra uno scalcinato muro!

Non domandarci la formula che mondi possa aprirti,
sì qualche storta sillaba e secca come un ramo.
Codesto solo oggi possiamo dirti,
ciò che *non* siamo, ciò che *non* vogliamo.

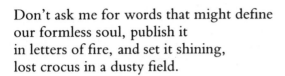

Don't ask me for words that might define
our formless soul, publish it
in letters of fire, and set it shining,
lost crocus in a dusty field.

Ah, that man so confidently striding,
friend to others and himself, careless
that the dog days' sun might stamp
his shadow on a crumbling wall!

Don't ask me for formulas to open worlds
for you: all I have are gnarled syllables,
branch-dry. All I can tell you now is this:
what we are *not,* what we do *not* want.

Meriggiare pallido e assorto
presso un rovente muro d'orto,
ascoltare tra i pruni e gli sterpi
schiocchi di merli, frusci di serpi.

Nelle crepe del suolo o su la veccia
spiar le file di rosse formiche
ch'ora si rompono ed ora s'intrecciano
a sommo di minuscole biche.

Osservare tra frondi il palpitare
lontano di scaglie di mare .
mentre si levano tremuli scricchi
di cicale dai calvi picchi.

E andando nel sole che abbaglia
sentire con triste meraviglia
com'è tutta la vita e il suo travaglio
in questo seguitare una muraglia
che ha in cima cocci aguzzi di bottiglia.

To laze at noon, pale and thoughtful,
by a blazing garden wall; to listen,
in brambles and brake, to blackbirds
scolding, the snake's rustle.

To gaze at the cracked earth, the leaves
of vetch, to spy the red ants filing past,
breaking, then twining, massing
at the tips of the tiny sheaves.

To peer through leaves at the sea,
scale on scale, pulsing in the distance,
while the cicada's quavering cry
shrills from naked peaks.

And then, walking out, dazed with light,
to sense with sad wonder
how all of life and its hard travail
is in this trudging along a wall spiked
with jagged shards of broken bottles.

Non rifugiarti nell'ombra
di quel fólto di verzura
come il falchetto che strapiomba
fulmineo nella caldura.

È ora di lasciare il canneto
stento che pare s'addorma
e di guardare le forme
della vita che si sgretola.

Ci muoviamo in un pulviscolo
madreperlaceo che vibra,
in un barbaglio che invischia
gli occhi e un poco ci sfibra.

Pure, lo senti, nel gioco d'aride onde
che impigra in quest'ora di disagio
non buttiamo già in un gorgo senza fondo
le nostre vite randage.

Come quella chiostra di rupi
che sembra sfilaccicarsi
in ragnatele di nubi;
tali i nostri animi arsi

in cui l'illusione brucia
un fuoco pieno di cenere
si perdono nel sereno
di una certezza: la luce.

Don't take shelter in the shade
of that green thicket,
like the windhover swooping, streak
of lightning in summer heat.

Time now to quit the canebrake
stricken as though with sleep
and gaze at the forms of a life
that powders away.

We pass in a shimmer of dust,
mother-of-pearl, a glare
that ensnares the eyes,
undoing us nearly.

Still, you sense it, in these dry waves
lazing in this hour of distress
let's not throw our strayed lives
to a bottomless abyss.

Like those enclosing cliffs
that seem to fray
in a webbing of haze,
so our charred souls

where illusion burns
in a flare of ash
vanish in the bright air
of one certainty: light.

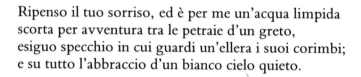

a K.

Ripenso il tuo sorriso, ed è per me un'acqua limpida
scorta per avventura tra le petraie d'un greto,
esiguo specchio in cui guardi un'ellera i suoi corimbi;
e su tutto l'abbraccio d'un bianco cielo quieto.

Codesto è il mio ricordo; non saprei dire, o lontano,
se dal tuo volto s'esprime libera un'anima ingenua,
o vero tu sei dei raminghi che il male del mondo estenua
e recano il loro soffrire con sé come un talismano.

Ma questo posso dirti, che la tua pensata effigie
sommerge i crucci estrosi in un'ondata di calma,
e che il tuo aspetto s'insinua nella mia memoria grigia
schietto come la cima d'una giovinetta palma . . .

I think again of your smile, a pool of limpid water
glimpsed by chance in the torrent's gravel bed,
a tiny mirror where ivy sees its clusters reflected,
embraced by a peaceful white sky overhead.

That I remember. O, distant one, I could not say
whether your face freely reveals a simple soul
or you are one of those restless ones wearied by the world's
evil, who wear their sufferings like an amulet.

But this I can say: the thought of your likeness
drowns my spasm of pain in tidal calm;
the candor of your image needles my dull memory
like the spear of a young palm. . . .

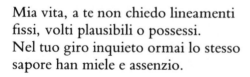

Mia vita, a te non chiedo lineamenti
fissi, volti plausibili o possessi.
Nel tuo giro inquieto ormai lo stesso
sapore han miele e assenzio.

Il cuore che ogni moto tiene a vile
raro è squassato da trasalimenti.
Così suona talvolta nel silenzio
della campagna un colpo di fucile.

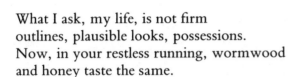

What I ask, my life, is not firm
outlines, plausible looks, possessions.
Now, in your restless running, wormwood
and honey taste the same.

The heart that loathes all motion
is seldom jolted by shocks.
So, at times, the country hush
is shattered by a shot.

Portami il girasole ch'io lo trapianti
nel mio terreno bruciato dal salino,
e mostri tutto il giorno agli azzurri specchianti
del cielo l'ansietà del suo volto giallino.

Tendono alla chiarità le cose oscure,
si esauriscono i corpi in un fluire
di tinte: queste in musiche. Svanire
è dunque la ventura delle venture.

Portami tu la pianta che conduce
dove sorgono bionde trasparenze
e vapora la vita quale essenza;
portami il girasole impazzito di luce.

Bring me the sunflower, I'll plant it here
in my patch of ground scorched by salt spume,
where all day long it will lift the craving
of its golden face to the mirroring blue.

Dark things are drawn to brighter,
bodies languish in a flowing
of colors, colors in musics. To vanish,
then, is the venture of ventures.

Bring me the flower that leads us out
where blond transparencies rise
and life evaporates as essence.
Bring me the sunflower crazed with light.

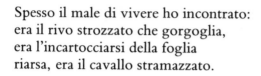

Spesso il male di vivere ho incontrato:
era il rivo strozzato che gorgoglia,
era l'incartocciarsi della foglia
riarsa, era il cavallo stramazzato.

Bene non seppi, fuori del prodigio
che schiude la divina Indifferenza:
era la statua nella sonnolenza
del meriggio, e la nuvola, e il falco alto levato.

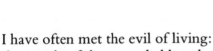

I have often met the evil of living:
the gurgle of the strangled brook,
the papering of the parched leaf,
the fallen horse, dying.

Of good I found little more than the omen
disclosed by the divine Indifference:
the statue in the drowsing
noon, and the cloud, and the hawk soaring.

Ciò che di me sapeste
non fu che la scialbatura,
la tonaca che riveste
la nostra umana ventura.

Ed era forse oltre il telo
l'azzurro tranquillo;
vietava il limpido cielo
solo un sigillo.

O vero c'era il falòtico
mutarsi della mia vita,
lo schiudersi d'un'ignita
zolla che mai vedrò.

Restò così questa scorza
la vera mia sostanza;
il fuoco che non si smorza
per me si chiamò: l'ignoranza.

Se un'ombra scorgete, non è
un'ombra—ma quella io sono.
Potessi spiccarla da me,
offrirvela in dono.

What you knew of me
was only a whitened skin,
the cowl that cloaks
our human destiny.

And perhaps behind the veil
the air was blue and still;
between me and the clear sky
lay a simple seal.

Or else it was that wildfire
changing of my life,
the disclosure of the kindled clod
I'll never see.

So then this husk remained
my true substance;
the name of unquenched fire
for me was—ignorance.

If you glimpse a shade,
it's not a shade—it's me.
If I could strip that shade away,
I'd give it to you, gladly.

Là fuoresce il Tritone
dai flutti che lambiscono
le soglie d'un cristiano
tempio, ed ogni ora prossima
è antica. Ogni dubbiezza
si conduce per mano
come una fanciulletta amica.

Là non è chi si guardi
o stia di sé in ascolto.
Quivi sei alle origini
e decidere è stolto:
ripartirai più tardi
per assumere un volto.

There Triton surges
from waves that lap
the sills of a Christian
shrine, and every future hour
is old. All hesitation
is taken by the hand
like a friendly little girl.

There no one regards himself
or heeds his own words.
Here you are at the sources,
decision is folly:
later you go home
and assume a face.

So l'ora in cui la faccia più impassibile
è traversata da una cruda smorfia:
s'è svelata per poco una pena invisibile.
Ciò non vede la gente nell'affollato corso.

Voi, mie parole, tradite invano il morso
secreto, il vento che nel cuore soffia.
La più vera ragione è di chi tace.
Il canto che singhiozza è un canto di pace.

I know that moment when a grimace of pain
crosses the most impassive face, briefly
revealing an anguish unseen
by people in the crowded street.

In vain, my words, you reveal the hidden
suffering, the wind gusting in the heart.
The real tale belongs to men of silence.
A song that weeps is a song of peace.

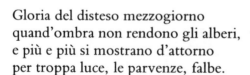

Gloria del disteso mezzogiorno
quand'ombra non rendono gli alberi,
e più e più si mostrano d'attorno
per troppa luce, le parvenze, falbe.

Il sole, in alto,—e un secco greto.
Il mio giorno non è dunque passato:
l'ora più bella è di là dal muretto
che rinchiude in un occaso scialbato.

L'arsura, in giro; un martin pescatore
volteggia s'una reliquia di vita.
La buona pioggia è di là dallo squallore,
ma in attendere è gioia più compita.

Splendor of noon outspread,
when trees cast no shadow, and more and more
excess of light gives to everything around
a tawny shimmer.

Above, the sun—and the dry shingle.
My day, then, isn't done. Not yet:
the loveliest hour lies beyond the wall
enclosing us in a wan sunset.

Drought all around: over a relic
of life a kingfisher hovering.
Beyond dejection lies the bliss of rain,
but happiness won is in the waiting.

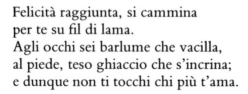

Felicità raggiunta, si cammina
per te su fil di lama.
Agli occhi sei barlume che vacilla,
al piede, teso ghiaccio che s'incrina;
e dunque non ti tocchi chi più t'ama.

Se giungi sulle anime invase
di tristezza e le schiari, il tuo mattino
è dolce e turbatore come i nidi delle cimase.
Ma nulla paga il pianto del bambino
a cui fugge il pallone tra le case.

Happiness won: for you we walk
the knife's edge.
The eyes see a flickering glow.
Underfoot thin ice cracks.
May he who loves you most never make you his.

If your brightness shines
on souls in sorrow, your mornings
are a joy, a fluttering like nests among the chimneys.
But what can console the crying child
whose balloon vanishes between the buildings?

Il canneto rispunta i suoi cimelli
nella serenità che non si ragna:
l'orto assetato sporge irti ramelli
oltre i chiusi ripari, all'afa stagna.

Sale un'ora d'attesa in cielo, vacua,
dal mare che s'ingrigia.
Un albero di nuvole sull'acqua
cresce, poi crolla come di cinigia.

Assente, come manchi in questa plaga
che ti presente e senza te consuma:
sei lontana e però tutto divaga
dal suo solco, dirupa, spare in bruma.

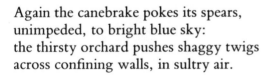

Again the canebrake pokes its spears,
unimpeded, to bright blue sky:
the thirsty orchard pushes shaggy twigs
across confining walls, in sultry air.

An hour of expectation rises skyward,
frustrated, from the sea that darkens.
Over the water a tree of clouds
branches up, then crumbles in ashes.

How this coast yearns for you in your absence,
intuits your coming, and wastes without it!
Lacking you, the world strays
from its course, plunges, vanishes in haze.

Forse un mattino andando in un'aria di vetro,
arida, rivolgendomi, vedrò compirsi il miracolo:
il nulla alle mie spalle, il vuoto dietro
di me, con un terrore di ubriaco.

Poi come s'uno schermo, s'accamperanno di gitto
alberi case colli per l'inganno consueto.
Ma sarà troppo tardi; ed io me n'andrò zitto
tra gli uomini che non si voltano, col mio segreto.

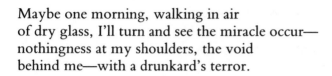

Maybe one morning, walking in air
of dry glass, I'll turn and see the miracle occur—
nothingness at my shoulders, the void
behind me—with a drunkard's terror.

Then, as on a screen, the usual illusion:
hills houses trees will suddenly reassemble,
but too late, and I'll quietly go my way,
with my secret, among men who don't look back.

Valmorbia, discorrevano il tuo fondo
fioriti nuvoli di piante agli àsoli.
Nasceva in noi, volti dal cieco caso,
oblio del mondo.

Tacevano gli spari, nel grembo solitario
non dava suono che il Leno roco.
Sbocciava un razzo su lo stelo, fioco
lacrimava nell'aria.

Le notti chiare erano tutte un'alba
e portavano volpi alla mia grotta.
Valmorbia, un nome—e ora nella scialba
memoria, terra dove non annotta.

Valmorbia, across your glens cloud-blossoms
scurried, wildflowers in the breezes.
In us, whirled by blind chance, oblivion
of the world was born.

The barrage stopped, in the lonely
vale no sound but the husky Leno.
A rocket sprouted on its stem, wailed
faintly through the air.

The bright nights, all one dawn,
led foxes to my cave.
Valmorbia, a name—and now, in my dim
memory, land that lightens.

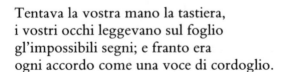

Tentava la vostra mano la tastiera,
i vostri occhi leggevano sul foglio
gl'impossibili segni; e franto era
ogni accordo come una voce di cordoglio.

Compresi che tutto, intorno, s'inteneriva
in vedervi inceppata inerme ignara
del linguaggio più vostro: ne bruiva
oltre i vetri socchiusi la marina chiara.

Passò nel riquadro azzurro una fugace danza
di farfalle; una fronda si scrollò nel sole.
Nessuna cosa prossima trovava le sue parole,
ed era mia, era *nostra,* la vostra dolce ignoranza.

Your hand was trying the keyboard,
your eyes were reading the impossible
signs on the score; and every chord
was suspended, like a voice grieving.

I felt everything around you go tender,
seeing you stop, helpless, ignorant
of the language most your own: beyond,
window ajar, bright water murmured back.

Butterflies danced, framed in blue, then
vanished; a bough shook in the sun.
Nothing, nothing around us, found words,
and your winsome ignorance was mine, was *ours*.

La farandola dei fanciulli sul greto
era la vita che scoppia dall'arsura.
Cresceva tra rare canne e uno sterpeto
il cespo umano nell'aria pura.

Il passante sentiva come un supplizio
il suo distacco dalle antiche radici.
Nell'età d'oro florida sulle sponde felici
anche un nome, una veste, erano un vizio.

The children's farandole along the shore
was life itself, exploding from drought.
Among a scattering of reeds and brush
the human plant leafed in the pure air.

Far from his ancient roots,
the passerby felt the torment of division.
In the golden age, on the shores of the blest,
even names, even clothes, were sin.

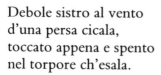

Debole sistro al vento
d'una persa cicala,
toccato appena e spento
nel torpore ch'esala.

Dirama dal profondo
in noi la vena
segreta: il nostro mondo
si regge appena.

Se tu l'accenni, all'aria
bigia treman corrotte
le vestigia
che il vuoto non ringhiotte.

Il gesto indi s'annulla,
tace ogni voce,
discende alla sua foce
la vita brulla.

Faint wind–borne sistrum
of a lost cicada, no sooner
shaken than spent,
in the breathing torpor.

The vein deep
inside us surges,
branching; our world
holds out, barely.

Make a gesture
and the gray air quivers
with decaying vestiges
the void rejects.

Then the gesture dies;
the voices fade; a waste
of debris, the torrent of life
plunges to the sea.

Cigola la carrucola del pozzo,
l'acqua sale alla luce e vi si fonde.
Trema un ricordo nel ricolmo secchio,
nel puro cerchio un'immagine ride.
Accosto il volto a evanescenti labbri:
si deforma il passato, si fa vecchio,
appartiene ad un altro . . .
                              Ah che già stride
la ruota, ti ridona all'atro fondo,
visione, una distanza ci divide.

The windlass creaks in the well,
the water rises, dissolves in light.
A memory quivers in the brimming pail;
in the pure circle an image laughs.
I bend my face to fleeting lips:
the past grows twisted, wrinkles with age,
belongs to someone else. . . .
Ah, but then a screech,
O vision, and the wheel slides you back to darkness,
riving you from me.

Arremba su la strinata proda
le navi di cartone, e dormi,
fanciulletto padrone: che non oda
tu i malevoli spiriti che veleggiano a stormi.

Nel chiuso dell'ortino svolacchia il gufo
e i fumacchi dei tetti sono pesi.
L'attimo che rovina l'opera lenta di mesi
giunge: ora incrina segreto, ora divelge in un buffo.

Viene lo spacco; forse senza strepito.
Chi ha edificato sente la sua condanna.
È l'ora che si salva solo la barca in panna.
Amarra la tua flotta tra le siepi.

Haul your paper boats
to the parched shore, and then to sleep,
little commodore: may you never hear
swarms of evil spirits putting in.

The owl flits in the walled orchard,
a pall of smoke lies heavy on the roof.
The moment that spoils months of labor is here:
now the secret crack, now the ravaging gust.

The crack widens, unheard perhaps.
The builder hears his sentence passed.
Now only the sheltered boat is safe.
Beach your fleet, secure it in the brush.

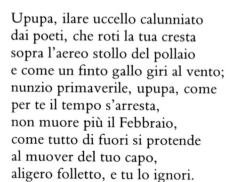

Upupa, ilare uccello calunniato
dai poeti, che roti la tua cresta
sopra l'aereo stollo del pollaio
e come un finto gallo giri al vento;
nunzio primaverile, upupa, come
per te il tempo s'arresta,
non muore più il Febbraio,
come tutto di fuori si protende
al muover del tuo capo,
aligero folletto, e tu lo ignori.

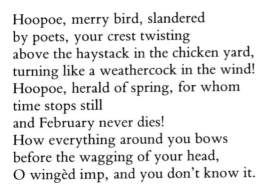

Hoopoe, merry bird, slandered
by poets, your crest twisting
above the haystack in the chicken yard,
turning like a weathercock in the wind!
Hoopoe, herald of spring, for whom
time stops still
and February never dies!
How everything around you bows
before the wagging of your head,
O wingèd imp, and you don't know it.

Sul muro grafito
che adombra i sedili rari
l'arco del cielo appare
finito.

Chi si ricorda più del fuoco ch'arse
impetuoso
nelle vene del mondo;—in un riposo
freddo le forme, opache, sono sparse.

Rivedrò domani le banchine
e la muraglia e l'usata strada.
Nel futuro che s'apre le mattine
sono ancorate come barche in rada.

Above the graffiti-covered wall
shading a few benches
the vault of heaven seems
ended.

Who still remembers the fire that blazed
with such ardor
in the world's veins? Now, in cold repose,
opaque, the forms are scattered.

Tomorrow I'll see the wharves again,
and the long wall and the traveled way.
In the future that begins, mornings
ride at anchor like boats in the bay.

Mediterranean

A vortice s'abbatte
sul mio capo reclinato
un suono d'agri lazzi.
Scotta la terra percorsa
da sghembe ombre di pinastri,
e al mare là in fondo fa velo
più che i rami, allo sguardo, l'afa che a tratti erompe
dal suolo che si avvena.
Quando più sordo o meno il ribollio dell'acque
che s'ingorgano
accanto a lunghe secche mi raggiunge:
o è un bombo talvolta ed un ripiovere
di schiume sulle rocce.
Come rialzo il viso, ecco cessare
i ragli sul mio capo; e via scoccare
verso le strepeanti acque,
frecciate biancazzurre, due ghiandaie.

A squall
of antic fleering swoops
above my bent head.
The ground, crisscrossed
by twisted shadows of wild pines, scorches.
Far below, the sea is hidden
by trees, but more by the veil of haze
fitfully vented by the cracking soil.
Louder, then muffled, the sound of seething
breakers strangled
by a long line of shoals reaches my ears:
or at times, a cloudburst of spume, exploding,
crashes on the cliffs.
I lift my gaze, suddenly the scolding stops; and down
to the boisterous waves streaks a flash
of blue-white arrows—
two jays.

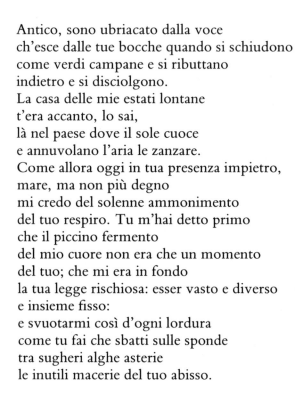

Antico, sono ubriacato dalla voce
ch'esce dalle tue bocche quando si schiudono
come verdi campane e si ributtano
indietro e si disciolgono.
La casa delle mie estati lontane
t'era accanto, lo sai,
là nel paese dove il sole cuoce
e annuvolano l'aria le zanzare.
Come allora oggi in tua presenza impietro,
mare, ma non più degno
mi credo del solenne ammonimento
del tuo respiro. Tu m'hai detto primo
che il piccino fermento
del mio cuore non era che un momento
del tuo; che mi era in fondo
la tua legge rischiosa: esser vasto e diverso
e insieme fisso:
e svuotarmi così d'ogni lordura
come tu fai che sbatti sulle sponde
tra sugheri alghe asterie
le inutili macerie del tuo abisso.

O Ancient, I am drunk on the voice
that breaks from your mouths when they unfold
like green bells, then collapse,
dissolving.
The house where I spent my summers long ago
stood, you know, at your side,
there in that land of searing sun where the air
goes hazy with mosquitoes.
O sea,
petrified by your presence then as now,
I think myself not worth the grave admonition
of your breath. You told me as a child
the petty ferment
of my heart was merely a moment
of yours; that your perilous law
lay deep within me: to be vast and various,
but unchanging too,
and so cleanse myself of every foulness.
You showed me how, hurling onto the beaches
sea-wrack starfish cork, all
the waste of your abyss.

Scendendo qualche volta
gli aridi greppi ormai
divisi dall'umoroso
Autunno che li gonfiava,
non m'era più in cuore la ruota
delle stagioni e il gocciare
del tempo inesorabile;
ma bene il presentimento
di te m'empiva l'anima,
sorpreso nell'ansimare
dell'aria, prima immota,
sulle rocce che orlavano il cammino.
Or, m'avvisavo, la pietra
voleva strapparsi, protesa
a un invisibile abbraccio;
la dura materia sentiva
il prossimo gorgo, e pulsava;
e i ciuffi delle avide canne
dicevano all'acque nascoste,
scrollando, un assentimento.
Tu vastità riscattavi
anche il patire dei sassi:
pel tuo tripudio era giusta
l'immobilità dei finiti.
Chinavo tra le petraie,
giungevano buffi salmastri
al cuore; era la tesa
del mare un giuoco di anella.
Con questa gioia precipita
dal chiuso vallotto alla spiaggia
la spersa pavoncella.

At times, climbing down
barren cliffs eroded
now and gorged
with autumn rains,
my heart no longer felt
the rhythm of the circling seasons,
the trickle of relentless time;
but the presentiment of you,
surprised in that heavy breathing
of air, before so still,
among the boulders bordering the path,
filled my soul.
Now, I thought, the very stone
was yearning to be free, to stretch
toward some invisible embrace;
hard matter intuited
the approaching gorge and quivered;
and the tufts of the reeds, eagerly
swaying, spoke assent
to the unseen waters.
O immensity, it was you, redeeming
even the stones in their suffering:
in your jubilation the fixity
of finite things was justified.
I was climbing down the scree.
Brackish winds came gusting
into my heart, the taut sea
was a game of quoits,
all gaiety, the joy
of the vagrant plover
mewed in the valley when she plummets
for the shore.

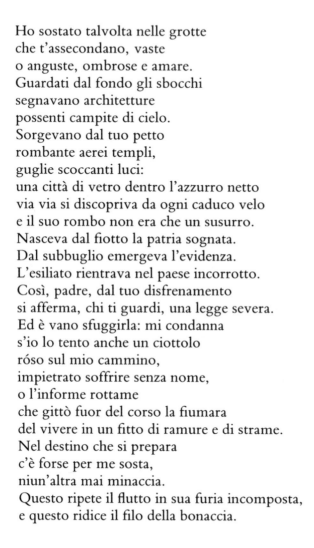

Ho sostato talvolta nelle grotte
che t'assecondano, vaste
o anguste, ombrose e amare.
Guardati dal fondo gli sbocchi
segnavano architetture
possenti campite di cielo.
Sorgevano dal tuo petto
rombante aerei templi,
guglie scoccanti luci:
una città di vetro dentro l'azzurro netto
via via si discopriva da ogni caduco velo
e il suo rombo non era che un susurro.
Nasceva dal fiotto la patria sognata.
Dal subbuglio emergeva l'evidenza.
L'esiliato rientrava nel paese incorrotto.
Così, padre, dal tuo disfrenamento
si afferma, chi ti guardi, una legge severa.
Ed è vano sfuggirla: mi condanna
s'io lo tento anche un ciottolo
róso sul mio cammino,
impietrato soffrire senza nome,
o l'informe rottame
che gittò fuor del corso la fiumara
del vivere in un fitto di ramure e di strame.
Nel destino che si prepara
c'è forse per me sosta,
niun'altra mai minaccia.
Questo ripete il flutto in sua furia incomposta,
e questo ridice il filo della bonaccia.

I have lingered at times
in grottoes at your side, vast
or cramped, dark, oppressive.
Viewed from within, their entrances
revealed imposing structures
against an expanse of sky.
From your thundering chest rose
ethereal temples,
spires darting lights:
in that bright blue a city of glass
slowly surfaced from the shrouding mist,
and its roar was merely a whisper.
Out of the sea rose the country I dreamed,
from turbulence the evidence arose.
The exile returned to his uncorrupted home.
So, father, your unchained fury
imposes a harsh command on your observer.
Evasion is hopeless; if I try,
even the salt-pocked stone
on my path condemns me—
a nameless, petrified patience,
or that chaos of debris
hurled aside by the torrent of life
in a litter of jumbled branches and straw.
In the destiny now forming
I may linger;
no other threat exists.
This, the restless rage of the surf keeps saying,
this, the whispering calm repeats.

Giunge a volte, repente,
un'ora che il tuo cuore disumano
ci spaura e dal nostro si divide.
Dalla mia la tua musica sconcorda,
allora, ed è nemico ogni tuo moto.
In me ripiego, vuoto
di forze, la tua voce pare sorda.
M'affisso nel pietrisco
che verso te digrada
fino alla ripa acclive che ti sovrasta,
franosa, gialla, solcata
da strosce d'acqua piovana.
Mia vita è questo secco pendio,
mezzo non fine, strada aperta a sbocchi
di rigagnoli, lento franamento.
È dessa, ancora, questa pianta
che nasce dalla devastazione
e in faccia ha i colpi del mare ed è sospesa
fra erratiche forze di venti.
Questo pezzo di suolo non erbato
s'è spaccato perché nascesse una margherita.
In lei titubo al mare che mi offende,
manca ancora il silenzio nella mia vita.
Guardo la terra che scintilla,
l'aria è tanto serena che s'oscura.
E questa che in me cresce
è forse la rancura
che ogni figliuolo, mare, ha per il padre.

Suddenly, at times, there comes
a moment when your inhuman heart,
estranged from ours, terrifies.
Then your music clashes with mine,
your every movement is hostile.
I withdraw into myself, drained
of strength, your voice is stifled.
I stare at the stony scree
spilling downhill toward you
to the bluff that slopes above you—
yellow, eroded, rutted
by rain-gouged torrents.
My life is this dry slope—
middle, not end—a road open to converging
runnels, one long, crumbling landslide.
It is this life, again, this flower,
devastation-born,
that dares the sea's hammering, sways
with the wind's capricious gusting.
In this patch of earth devoid of growing things,
a crack widens to let a daisy sprout.
In this flower I tremble toward the sea that lashes me;
silence is still an absence in my life.
I look at the earth, which glitters,
air so still it darkens.
And what grows in me
may be the rancor,
O sea, that every son feels for his father.

Noi non sappiamo quale sortiremo
domani, oscuro o lieto;
forse il nostro cammino
a non tócche radure ci addurrà
dove mormori eterna l'acqua di giovinezza;
o sarà forse un discendere
fino al vallo estremo,
nel buio, perso il ricordo del mattino.
Ancora terre straniere
forse ci accoglieranno: smarriremo
la memoria del sole, dalla mente
ci cadrà il tintinnare delle rime.
Oh la favola onde s'esprime
la nostra vita, repente
si cangerà nella cupa storia che non si racconta!
Pur di una cosa ci affidi,
padre, e questa è: che un poco del tuo dono
sia passato per sempre nelle sillabe
che rechiamo con noi, api ronzanti.
Lontani andremo e serberemo un'eco
della tua voce, come si ricorda
del sole l'erba grigia
nelle corti scurite, tra le case.
E un giorno queste parole senza rumore
che teco educammo nutrite
di stanchezze e di silenzi,
parranno a un fraterno cuore
sapide di sale greco.

What tomorrow will bring, joyful
or somber, no one knows.
Our road may take us
to clearings untrodden by human foot,
to whispering streams of eternal youth;
or perhaps a last descent
into that final valley,
all darkness, memory of light quite lost.
Foreign lands perhaps
will welcome us once more: we will lose
the memory of our sun, our lilting rhymes
will be forgotten.
And the fable
that expresses our lives will suddenly become
that grim tale no man will ever tell.
Still, O father, one legacy
you leave us: some small part of your genius
lives on in these syllables we bear with us,
humming bees.
However far our journey, we will always keep
an echo of your voice, like the brown grass
in dark courtyards between the houses,
which never forgets the light.
And a day will come when these unvoiced words,
seeded in us by you, nourished
on silence and fatigue,
will, to some brotherly soul, seem seasoned
with salt-sea brine.

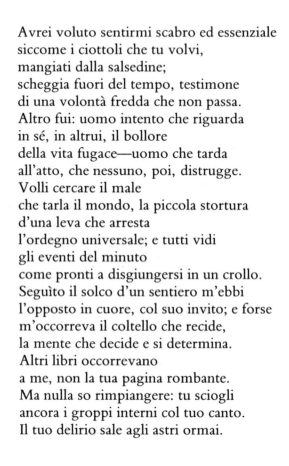

Avrei voluto sentirmi scabro ed essenziale
siccome i ciottoli che tu volvi,
mangiati dalla salsedine;
scheggia fuori del tempo, testimone
di una volontà fredda che non passa.
Altro fui: uomo intento che riguarda
in sé, in altrui, il bollore
della vita fugace—uomo che tarda
all'atto, che nessuno, poi, distrugge.
Volli cercare il male
che tarla il mondo, la piccola stortura
d'una leva che arresta
l'ordegno universale; e tutti vidi
gli eventi del minuto
come pronti a disgiungersi in un crollo.
Seguìto il solco d'un sentiero m'ebbi
l'opposto in cuore, col suo invito; e forse
m'occorreva il coltello che recide,
la mente che decide e si determina.
Altri libri occorrevano
a me, non la tua pagina rombante.
Ma nulla so rimpiangere: tu sciogli
ancora i groppi interni col tuo canto.
Il tuo delirio sale agli astri ormai.

I would have liked to feel rough, elemental
as the pebbles you tumble about,
pocked by salt,
a timeless shard, witness
to a cold, persistent will. I was
anything but: a man intent
on observing, in himself, and others, the furor
of fleeting life; a man who defers
doing, which therefore can never be undone.
I chose to search out the evil
gnawing at the world, the little warp
in the lever that locks
the universal gears; and I saw
all the events of the instant
as though poised to collapse and crumble.
I walked the road in one direction, while my heart
yearned for the other; and maybe
I needed the knife that slices through,
the mind that decides and determines.
I needed other
texts, not your thundering page.
But I have no regrets: once more
your song undoes my inward knots.
And now your frenzy rises to the stars.

Potessi almeno costringere
in questo mio ritmo stento
qualche poco del tuo vaneggiamento;
dato mi fosse accordare
alle tue voci il mio balbo parlare:—
io che sognava rapirti
le salmastre parole
in cui natura ed arte si confondono,
per gridar meglio la mia malinconia
di fanciullo invecchiato che non doveva pensare.
Ed invece non ho che le lettere fruste
dei dizionari, e l'oscura
voce che amore detta s'affioca,
si fa lamentosa letteratura.
Non ho che queste parole
che come donne pubblicate
s'offrono a chi le richiede;
non ho che queste frasi stancate
che potranno rubarmi anche domani
gli studenti canaglie in versi veri.
Ed il tuo rombo cresce, e si dilata
azzurra l'ombra nuova.
M'abbandonano a prova i miei pensieri.
Sensi non ho; né senso. Non ho limite.

If only I could force
some fragment of your ecstasy
into this clumsy music of mine;
had I the talent to match your voices
with my stammering speech—
I who once dreamed of acquiring
those salt-sea words of yours
where nature fuses with art—
and with your vast language proclaim the sadness
of an aging boy who shouldn't have learned to think.
But moldy dictionary words
are all I have, and that voice of mystery
dictated by love grows faint,
turns literary, elegiac.
All I have are these words
that, like public women,
offer themselves to any takers;
all I have are these clichés
which student rabble might tomorrow steal
in real poetry.
And your booming grows, and the blue
of the fresh shadow widens.
My thoughts fail, they leave me.
I have no sense, no senses. No limit.

Dissipa tu se lo vuoi
questa debole vita che si lagna,
come la spugna il frego
effimero di una lavagna.
M'attendo di ritornare nel tuo circolo,
s'adempia lo sbandato mio passare.
La mia venuta era testimonianza
di un ordine che in viaggio mi scordai,
giurano fede queste mie parole
a un evento impossibile, e lo ignorano.
Ma sempre che traudii
la tua dolce risacca su le prode
sbigottimento mi prese
quale d'uno scemato di memoria
quando si risovviene del suo paese.
Presa la mia lezione
più che dalla tua gloria
aperta, dall'ansare
che quasi non dà suono
di qualche tuo meriggio desolato,
a te mi rendo in umiltà. Non sono
che favilla d'un tirso. Bene lo so: bruciare,
questo, non altro, è il mio significato.

Squander, if you want,
this feeble, self-pitying life,
like a sponge wiping
a fleeting scrawl from the slate.
My lost bearings corrected,
I expect to reenter your orbit;
there let my wandering course
find consummation.
My coming was witness to an order
I forgot while on my way:
these words of mine swear allegiance
to an impossible event
of which they are ignorant.
But whenever I half-heard
your soft backwash on the shore,
I was shaken
like a man with failing memory
who remembers his native land.
From your manifest splendor
I have learned my lesson,
but that deep, almost inaudible
breathing of your desolate noons
taught me more. Humbly
I commit myself to you. I am nothing
but the spark of a thyrsus. I know it well: burning—
this, and only this, is my meaning.

Noons and Shadows

Fine dell'infanzia

Rombando s'ingolfava
dentro l'arcuata ripa
un mare pulsante, sbarrato da solchi,
cresputo e fioccoso di spume.
Di contro alla foce
d'un torrente che straboccava
il flutto ingialliva.
Giravano al largo i grovigli dell'alighe
e tronchi d'alberi alla deriva.

Nella conca ospitale
della spiaggia
non erano che poche case
di annosi mattoni, scarlatte,
e scarse capellature
di tamerici pallide
più d'ora in ora; stente creature
perdute in un orrore di visioni.
Non era lieve guardarle
per chi leggeva in quelle
apparenze malfide
la musica dell'anima inquieta
che non si decide.

Pure colline chiudevano d'intorno
marina e case; ulivi le vestivano
qua e là disseminati come greggi,
o tenui come il fumo di un casale
che veleggi
la faccia candente del cielo.

End of Childhood

Roaring, a throbbing sea
ploughed by giant furrows
and flaked with seething foam
flooded the half-moon of the bay.
Where it met the mouth
of a mountain torrent in spate,
the tide turned yellowish,
tangles of seaweed and trees grinding
wildly on the waves.

The genial shell
of the beach
held only a cluster of houses,
scarlet, built of old brick,
and a thin chevelure
of tamarisks growing paler
by the hour; stunted creatures
lost in a horror of visions.
No friendly sight,
not to a boy who reads in those
diffident shapes
the music of a restless,
undecided soul.

But houses and coast nestled
in hills dressed with olive trees
scattered here and there like flocks
or wisps of smoke from a farmhouse
drifting across
the shining face of the sky.

Tra macchie di vigneti e di pinete,
petraie si scorgevano
calve e gibbosi dorsi
di collinette: un uomo
che là passasse ritto s'un muletto
nell'azzurro lavato era stampato
per sempre—e nel ricordo.

Poco s'andava oltre i crinali prossimi
di quei monti; varcarli pur non osa
la memoria stancata.
So che strade correvano su fossi
incassati, tra garbugli di spini;
mettevano a radure, poi tra botri,
e ancora dilungavano
verso recessi madidi di muffe,
d'ombre coperti e di silenzi.
Uno ne penso ancora con meraviglia
dove ogni umano impulso
appare seppellito
in aura millenaria.
Rara diroccia qualche bava d'aria
sino a quell'orlo di mondo che ne strabilia.

Ma dalle vie del monte si tornava.
Riuscivano queste a un'instabile
vicenda d'ignoti aspetti
ma il ritmo che li governa ci sfuggiva.
Ogni attimo bruciava
negl'istanti futuri senza tracce.
Vivere era ventura troppo nuova
ora per ora, e ne batteva il cuore.
Norma non v'era,
solco fisso, confronto,
a sceverare gioia da tristezza.
Ma riaddotti dai viottoli
alla casa sul mare, al chiuso asilo
della nostra stupita fanciullezza,
rapido rispondeva
a ogni moto dell'anima un consenso

Amid splotches of vineyards, pines,
and outcropping ledge,
loomed bald, hunchbacked
hills; a man
passing on a mule
was stamped forever on that laundered
blue—and etched in memory too.

We rarely crossed the nearest ridges
of those peaks; even now our memory, exhausted,
lacks the courage to cross them.
I know there were paths that cut along steep
slopes, through thickets of briars,
then opened onto clearings, skirted ravines
and lengthened out
toward yawning caverns dank with mold,
sealed in silence and shadow.
Awed, I still remember one cleft
where every human impulse
seems buried
in stale millennia. Now and then
a few breaths of fresh air
trickled down, astounding
that rim of the world.

But we came back home from those mountain paths.
For us they became a flickering
alternation of strange realities,
but governed by an elusive rhythm.
Each instant, burning
into future instants, left no trace.
Just being alive was adventure, fresh, too fresh,
hour by hour, and the heart racing, always faster.
There were no rules,
no measure, no sure way
of dividing joy from sadness.
But when those country paths brought us home
to the house by the sea, to the cozy shelter
of our wide-eyed childhood,
a consensus beyond us

esterno, si vestivano di nomi
le cose, il nostro mondo aveva un centro.

Eravamo nell'età verginale
in cui le nubi non sono cifre o sigle
ma le belle sorelle che si guardano viaggiare.
D'altra semenza uscita
d'altra linfa nutrita
che non la nostra, debole, pareva la natura.
In lei l'asilo, in lei
l'estatico affisare; ella il portento
cui non sognava, o a pena, di raggiungere
l'anima nostra confusa.
Eravamo nell'età illusa.

Volarono anni corti come giorni,
sommerse ogni certezza un mare florido
e vorace che dava ormai l'aspetto
dubbioso dei tremanti tamarischi.
Un'alba dové sorgere che un rigo
di luce su la soglia
forbita ci annunziava come un'acqua;
e noi certo corremmo
ad aprire la porta
stridula sulla ghiaia del giardino.
L'inganno ci fu palese.
Pesanti nubi sul torbato mare
che ci bolliva in faccia, tosto apparvero.
Era in aria l'attesa
di un procelloso evento.
Strania anch'essa la plaga
dell'infanzia che esplora
un segnato cortile come un mondo!
Giungeva anche per noi l'ora che indaga.
La fanciullezza era morta in un giro a tondo.

Ah il giuoco dei cannibali nel canneto,
i mustacchi di palma, la raccolta
deliziosa dei bossoli sparati!
Volava la bella età come i barchetti sul filo

instantly responded
to every stirring of the soul,
things were clothed with names,
our world was centered.

Ours was that virginal age
when clouds are neither ciphers or symbols
but beautiful sisters, you watched them going by.
Nature seemed sprung
from a different seed, nourished
by a different lymph, far stronger than our own.
She was our refuge, we gazed at her in ecstasy;
she was the miracle our troubled soul dreamed,
or almost dreamed, of touching.
Such was our innocence.

Years, like days, went racing by,
all certainty swallowed by a sea
so vivid and ravenous it seemed tentative
as the trembling tamarisks.
Dawn was bound to come, heralded
by a sunburst on the shining
lintel. It broke like a great wave.
And we of course ran to open
the door that creaked on the gravel
leading to the garden.
The illusion stood revealed.
Suddenly over the wild water seething
at our feet, thick cloudpack appeared.
Expectation of a storm
filled the air.
All so strange—even that parish of childhood
which explored the homey courtyard
as though it were the world, receded!
For us too the time had come for asking questions.
Our childhood died in a roundelay.

Ah, playing at cannibals in the canebrake,
palm-leaf mustachios, sweet
harvesting of cartridge shells!

III

del mare a vele colme.
Certo guardammo muti nell'attesa
del minuto violento;
poi nella finta calma
sopra l'acque scavate
dové mettersi un vento.

Like sailboats running free along the horizon
of the sea, the happy years slid away.
Naturally we watched, silent, waiting for the violence
to strike;
now, in that deceptive calm
on the yawning swells,
a wind no doubt
was kicking up.

L'AGAVE SU LO SCOGLIO

Scirocco

O rabido ventare di scirocco
che l'arsiccio terreno gialloverde
bruci;
e su nel cielo pieno
di smorte luci
trapassa qualche biocco
di nuvola, e si perde.
Ore perplesse, brividi
d'una vita che fugge
come acqua tra le dita;
inafferrati eventi,
luci-ombre, commovimenti
delle cose malferme della terra;
oh alide ali dell'aria
ora son io
l'agave che s'abbarbica al crepaccio
dello scoglio
e sfugge al mare da le braccia d'alghe
che spalanca ampie gole e abbranca rocce;
e nel fermento
d'ogni essenza, coi miei racchiusi bocci
che non sanno più esplodere oggi sento
la mia immobilità come un tormento.

AGAVE ON THE CLIFF

Scirocco

O scirocco, rabid gale
that parches
the cracked green-yellow ground;
and high above, thick
with livid flashes,
a few wisps of cloud
scud past and vanished.
Baffled hours, tremors
of a life that slips away,
water through fingers;
unapprehended events,
shadow-lights, quakings
of earth's unstable things;
O stifling wings of air
now I am
the agave that hugs the crevice
in the cliff,
flinches from seaweed arms groping
from the surf, jaws agape, clawing at the rocks;
and in that seething
of every essence, my buds clenched tight,
incapable of breaking into bloom, today I feel
this rootedness of mine
is torture.

Ed ora sono spariti i circoli d'ansia
che discorrevano il lago del cuore
e quel friggere vasto della materia
che discolora e muore.
Oggi una volontà di ferro spazza l'aria,
divelle gli arbusti, strapazza i palmizi
e nel mare compresso scava
grandi solchi crestati di bava.
Ogni forma si squassa nel subbuglio
degli elementi; è un urlo solo, un muglio
di scerpate esistenze: tutto schianta
l'ora che passa: viaggiano la cupola del cielo
non sai se foglie o uccelli—e non son più.
E tu che tutta ti scrolli fra i tonfi
dei venti disfrenati
e stringi a te i bracci gonfi
di fiori non ancora nati;
come senti nemici
gli spiriti che la convulsa terra
sorvolano a sciami,
mia vita sottile, e come ami
oggi le tue radici.

And now they're gone, those anxious
circles that pattered across the lake of my heart,
and with them went that huge sputtering of matter
whose colors leach and die.
Today a will of iron flails the skies,
uproots the shrubs, batters the palms,
and scoops huge foaming furrows
from the savaged sea.
In elemental chaos all forms
pitch and reel—one huge howl, a clamor
of blasted lives. All things are shaken
by the passing hour. Birds—leaves?—
streak across the vault of the sky and vanish.
And you, all asway in that buffeting
of winds unbridled,
hug those branches
great with blossoms almost born. O my slim-stalked
life, how alien they seem, these ghosts
that flash past, swarming
over earth's agony,
how dearly you love these roots of yours
today.

S'è rifatta la calma
nell'aria: tra gli scogli parlotta la maretta.
Sulla costa quietata, nei broli, qualche palma
a pena svetta.

Una carezza disfiora
la linea del mare e la scompiglia
un attimo, soffio lieve che vi s'infrange e ancora
il cammino ripiglia.

Lameggia nella chiaria
la vasta distesa, s'increspa, indi si spiana beata
e specchia nel suo cuore vasto codesta povera mia
vita turbata.

O mio tronco che additi,
in questa ebrietudine tarda,
ogni rinato aspetto coi germogli fioriti
sulle tue mani, guarda:

sotto l'azzurro fitto
del cielo qualche uccello di mare se ne va;
né sosta mai: perché tutte le immagini portano scritto:
'più in là!'.

Now the calm returns, the air
is still; waves chatter with the reefs.
In gardens on the quiet coast, palm leaves
barely quiver.

A caress skims
the line of the sea, briefly
ruffling, a soft breath that breaks off, then
slides away.

The vast expanse
billows in the brightness, wrinkles, subsides—
serene, a giant heart that reflects my life,
petty, unsatisfied.

O my stalk, you
whose arms, all bursting blossoms
now reveal rebirth
in everything, look:

beneath the dense blue
sky, seabirds flash by, never
pausing, driven by images below:
"Farther, farther!"

Vasca

Passò sul tremulo vetro
un riso di belladonna fiorita,
di tra le rame urgevano le nuvole,
dal fondo ne riassommava
la vista fioccosa e sbiadita.
Alcuno di noi tirò un ciottolo
che ruppe la tesa lucente:
le molli parvenze s'infransero.

Ma ecco, c'è altro che striscia
a fior della spera rifatta liscia:
di erompere non ha virtù,
vuol vivere e non sa come;
se lo guardi si stacca, torna in giù:
è nato e morto, e non ha avuto un nome.

Pool

A smile of belladonna in bloom
brushed the quivering glass,
clouds were prying between the branches,
a pale, tufted reflection
rose from below.
One of us tossed a pebble, tearing
the taut film of bright water:
the soft apparitions shattered.

But look, there: something else, a slither
skimming the recomposèd mirror:
it lacks the strength to emerge:
it wants to live and doesn't know how;
it shrinks from your gaze, and drowns:
it was born, and died, it had no name.

Egloga

Perdersi nel bigio ondoso
dei miei ulivi era buono
nel tempo andato—loquaci
di riottanti uccelli
e di cantanti rivi.
Come affondava il tallone
nel suolo screpolato,
tra le lamelle d'argento
dell'esili foglie. Sconnessi
nascevano in mente i pensieri
nell'aria di troppa quiete.

Ora è finito il cerulo marezzo.
Si getta il pino domestico
a romper la grigiura;
brucia una toppa di cielo
in alto, un ragnatelo
si squarcia al passo: si svincola
d'attorno un'ora fallita.
È uscito un rombo di treno,
non lunge, ingrossa. Uno sparo
si schiaccia nell'etra vetrino.
Strepita un volo come un acquazzone,
venta e vanisce bruciata
una bracciata di amara
tua scorza, istante: discosta
esplode furibonda una canea.

Tosto potrà rinascere l'idillio.
S'è ricomposta la fase che pende
dal cielo, riescono bende
leggere fuori . . . ;
                il fitto dei fagiuoli

Eclogue

Losing myself in the swaying gray
of my olives garrulous
with quarreling birds
and freshets singing—
how good it used to be!
How the heel sank
in the cracked earth
among tiny blades of thin-leaved
silver! Random
thoughts came springing to mind
in that air too still.

Now the watered blue is gone.
The family pine leaps out,
breaking the grisaille;
overhead a patch of sky
burns, a spiderweb
is torn by a passing step: all around
a lost hour sheds its chains.
Nearby, the roar of a train
begins, then swells. A shot
cracks in the glassy air.
A flock of birds, a cloudburst,
crashes past, O Instant, an armful
of your bitter bark, ashes
blow by, vanish: the distance explodes,
a furious baying.

Soon the idyll can be reborn.
The phase that depends on the sky
is recomposed; streamers
struggle free . . . ;
    the thicket of beans

n'è scancellato e involto.
Non serve più rapid'ale,
né giova proposito baldo;
non durano che le solenni cicale
in questi saturnali del caldo.
Va e viene un istante in un folto
una parvenza di donna.
È disparsa, non era una Baccante.

Sul tardi corneggia la luna.
Ritornavamo dai nostri
vagabondari infruttuosi.
Non si leggeva più in faccia
al mondo la traccia
della frenesia durata
il pomeriggio. Turbati
discendevamo tra i vepri.
Nei miei paesi a quell'ora
cominciano a fischiare le lepri.

is erased, folded in haze.
Swift wings no longer serve,
boldness of purpose is no help;
only the grave cicadas endure
in these Saturnalias of heat.
For an instant in the thick scrub
a woman's apparition flickers,
then vanishes. No Maenad, she.

Later on the moon lifts her horns.
This was when we came back home
from our useless wanderings.
On the face of the world
no trace could be found
of the wild orgy that lasted
all afternoon. Troubled,
we'd walk down among the thistles.
Where I live that's the time
when the hares begin to whistle.

Flussi

I fanciulli con gli archetti
spaventano gli scriccioli nei buchi.
Cola il pigro sereno nel riale
che l'accidia sorrade,
pausa che gli astri donano ai malvivi
camminatori delle bianche strade.
Alte tremano guglie di sambuchi
e sovrastano al poggio
cui domina una statua dell'Estate
fatta camusa da lapidazioni;
e su lei cresce un roggio
di rampicanti ed un ronzio di fuchi.
Ma la dea mutilata non s'affaccia
e ogni cosa si tende alla flottiglia
di carta che discende lenta il vallo.
Brilla in aria una freccia,
si configge s'un palo, oscilla tremula.
La vita è questo scialo
di triti fatti, vano
più che crudele.
                    Tornano
le tribù dei fanciulli con le fionde
se è scorsa una stagione od un minuto,
e i morti aspetti scoprono immutati
se pur tutto è diruto
e più dalla sua rama non dipende
il frutto conosciuto.
—Ritornano i fanciulli . . . ; così un giorno
il giro che governa
la nostra vita ci addurrà il passato
lontano, franto e vivido, stampato
sopra immobili tende
da un'ignota lanterna.—

Flux

Boys with snares
scare the wrens back to their nests.
Sluggish blue sky trickles into the brook
coated with accidie—
respite granted by the stars to those poor wretches
who walk the white roads.
Spires of elders shiver
on the hilltop dominated
by a statue of goddess Summer
nose chipped away by volleys of stones,
body overgrown by a russet
of vines, a droning of bees.
But the vandalized goddess is withdrawn
and everything reaches out to the flotilla
of paper boats slowly drifting downstream.
An arrow stabs the air,
impales a post, sways and quivers.
Life is this squandered waste
of everyday events, more futile
than cruel.
       Tribes of boys
armed with slingshots keep returning,
every minute, every season,
and dead aspects are revealed unchanged,
though everything is ruined,
and familiar fruit no longer
hangs from the branch.
—The boys return. . . . So too, someday,
the cycle that controls our life
will lead us back to that distant past,
its vivid shards printed
by an unknown lantern
on curtains that do not stir.—

E ancora si distende
un dòmo celestino ed appannato
sul fitto bulicame del fossato:
e soltanto la statua
sa che il tempo precipita e s'infrasca
vie più nell'accesa edera.
E tutto scorre nella gran discesa
e fiotta il fosso impetuoso tal che
s'increspano i suoi specchi:
fanno naufragio i piccoli sciabecchi
nei gorghi dell'acquiccia insaponata.
Addio!—fischiano pietre tra le fronde,
la rapace fortuna è già lontana,
cala un'ora, i suoi volti riconfonde,—
e la vita è crudele più che vana.

And the blue blur of a heavenly dome
still vaults the thick scum
coating the ditch; and only the statue knows
that time is plunging past, and wreathes herself
deeper still in the scarlet blaze of the ivy.
And all things race by in the huge descent,
and the ditch seethes and surges
till its pools wrinkle:
and paper schooners founder
in riptides of lather.
Farewell!—stones go whistling through the leaves,
ravening fortune is nowhere near;
an hour sets, recomposes its features,—
and life is more cruel than futile.

Clivo

Viene un suono di buccine
dal greppo che scoscende,
discende verso il mare
che tremola e si fende per accoglierlo.
Cala nella ventosa gola
con l'ombre la parola
che la terra dissolve sui frangenti;
si dismemora il mondo e può rinascere.
Con le barche dell'alba
spiega la luce le sue grandi vele
e trova stanza in cuore la speranza.
Ma ora lungi è il mattino,
sfugge il chiarore e s'aduna
sovra eminenze e frondi,
e tutto è più raccolto e più vicino
come visto a traverso di una cruna;
ora è certa la fine,
e s'anche il vento tace
senti la lima che sega
assidua la catena che ci lega.

Come una musicale frana
divalla il suono, s'allontana.
Con questo si disperdono le accolte
voci dalle volute
aride dei crepacci;
il gemito delle pendìe,
là tra le viti che i lacci
delle radici stringono.
Il clivo non ha più vie,
le mani s'afferrano ai rami
dei pini nani; poi trema
e scema il bagliore del giorno;

Slope

A blare of trumpets breaks
from the sheer cliff that falls away,
spilling toward the sea
that shivers and splinters to take it in.
Down in the windy gorge among shadows
plummets the word
which the earth dissolves on the breakers;
the world loses all memory, the world can be
reborn. With the boats at dawn
light unfurls its great sails,
hope finds room in the heart.
But now morning is long past,
the brightness melts, to gather again
on heights and leaves,
and all things shrink, compacted,
as though viewed through the eye of a needle;
the end is certain now,
and when the wind is still,
you hear the assiduous file sawing
at the chain that binds us.

The sound cascades, a landslide
of music, then fades.
And as it dies, voices
gathered in the parched
whorls of the cliff disperse
with the groaning of the slopes
there among the vines
clenched hard by twining roots.
Paths on the cliff buckle,
hands clutch at branches
of stunted pines; the day's
splendor quivers and wanes;

e un ordine discende che districa
dai confini
le cose che non chiedono
ormai che di durare, di persistere
contente dell'infinita fatica;
un crollo di pietrame che dal cielo
s'inabissa alle prode . . .

Nella sera distesa appena, s'ode
un ululo di corni, uno sfacelo.
e un ordine discende che districa
dai confini
le cose che non chiedono
ormai che di durare, di persistere
contente dell'infinita fatica;
un crollo di pietrame che dal cielo
s'inabissa alle prode . . .

Nella sera distesa appena, s'ode
un ululo di corni, uno sfacelo.

and an order descends,
freeing from their limits
things that now demand
only to persist, endure,
content with their infinite toil;
a sudden rockslide from the sky
plunging to the shore. . . .

In the evening that now widens, a squalling
of horns is heard. A dissolution.

Arsenio

I turbini sollevano la polvere
sui tetti, a mulinelli, e sugli spiazzi
deserti, ove i cavalli incappucciati
annusano la terra, fermi innanzi
ai vetri luccicanti degli alberghi.
Sul corso, in faccia al mare, tu discendi
in questo giorno
or piovorno ora acceso, in cui par scatti
a sconvolgerne l'ore
uguali, strette in trama, un ritornello
di castagnette.

È il segno d'un'altra orbita: tu seguilo.
Discendi all'orizzonte che sovrasta
una tromba di piombo, alta sui gorghi,
più d'essi vagabonda: salso nembo
vorticante, soffiato dal ribelle
elemento alle nubi; fa che il passo
su la ghiaia ti scriccholi e t'inciampi
il viluppo dell'alghe: quell'istante
è forse, molto atteso, che ti scampi
dal finire il tuo viaggio, anello d'una
catena, immoto andare, oh troppo noto
delirio, Arsenio, d'immobilità . . .

Ascolta tra i palmizi il getto tremulo
dei violini, spento quando rotola
il tuono con un fremer di lamiera
percossa; la tempesta è dolce quando
sgorga bianca la stella di Canicola

Arsenio

Eddying squalls raise the dust
over roofs and deserted
spaces, where blinkered horses,
stockstill, sniff the ground
before the glistening windows of hotels.
On the promenade facing the sea, you descend
on this day
of alternating sun and rain, the taut weave
of hours too much alike torn
by what seems an occasional
burst of castanets.

Sign of another orbit: follow it.
Descend to the horizon where a leaden
waterspout hangs in the sky over the whitecaps,
more restless than they: a brackish
whirlwind spumed by the rebel element
against the clouds; let your footstep
crunch on gravel and stumble
in tangled seaweed: maybe
this is the moment, so long awaited,
that frees you from your journey, link
in a chain, unmoving motion, ah, that too familiar
ecstasy, Arsenio, of inertia. . . .

Listen, among the palms, to the tremolo spurt
of violins, quenched by the rolling
thunder, like sheet metal
clanging; the storm is sweet
when the Dog Star shows, white

nel cielo azzurro e lunge par la sera
ch'è prossima: se il fulmine la incide
dirama come un albero prezioso
entro la luce che s'arrosa: e il timpano
degli tzigani è il rombo silenzioso.

Discendi in mezzo al buio che precipita
e muta il mezzogiorno in una notte
di globi accesi, dondolanti a riva,—
e fuori, dove un'ombra sola tiene
mare e cielo, dai gozzi sparsi palpita
l'acetilene—
              finché goccia trepido
il cielo, fuma il suolo che s'abbevera,
tutto d'accanto ti sciaborda, sbattono
le tende molli, un frùscio immenso rade
la terra, giù s'afflosciano stridendo
le lanterne di carta sulle strade.

Così sperso tra i vimini e le stuoie
grondanti, giunco tu che le radici
con sé trascina, viscide, non mai
svelte, tremi di vita e ti protendi
a un vuoto risonante di lamenti
soffocati, la tesa ti ringhiotte
dell'onda antica che ti volge; e ancora
tutto che ti riprende, strada portico
mura specchi ti figge in una sola
ghiacciata moltitudine di morti,
e se un gesto ti sfiora, una parola
ti cade accanto, quello è forse, Arsenio,
nell'ora che si scioglie, il cenno d'una
vita strozzata per te sorta, e il vento
la porta con la cenere degli astri.

in the blue sky and the nearing night
seems so far away: lightning-splintered,
it branches out like some jeweled tree
in the light that reddens: and the gypsy
tambour is the rumble of silence.

Descend into that sheer darkness rushing down
that changes midday into a night
of blazing globes swaying on the bank,—
and beyond, there where a single shadow
holds sea and sky, from scattered fishing boats
acetylene torches throb—
                                        until the sky
shivers into drops, and the dank earth steams,
everything around you spills over, the drooping
awnings flap, a huge flurry
brushes the earth; hissing,
the paper lanterns fall soggy to the streets.

So, lost among wicker and drenched
mats, a reed dragging its roots, all slime,
never torn up, quivering with life,
you lean out toward an emptiness loud
with stifled grief, the crest
of the ancient wave in which you tumble
swallows you again; and once again
all things seize you, street, arcades,
mirrors, walls, fixing you in a single
frozen multitude of the dead,
and should one gesture graze you, one word
fall at your side, perhaps, Arsenio,
in the hour dissolving, this is the call
of some strangled life that emerged on your behalf,
and the wind whirls it away with the ashes of the stars.

Crisalide

L'albero verdecupo
si stria di giallo tenero e s'ingromma.
Vibra nell'aria una pietà per l'avide
radici, per le tumide cortecce.
Son vostre queste piante
scarse che si rinnovano
all'alito d'Aprile, umide e liete.
Per me che vi contemplo da quest'ombra,
altro cespo riverdica, e voi siete.

Ogni attimo vi porta nuove fronde
e il suo sbigottimento avanza ogni altra
gioia fugace; viene a impetuose onde
la vita a questo estremo angolo d'orto.
Lo sguardo ora vi cade su le zolle;
una risacca di memorie giunge
al vostro cuore e quasi lo sommerge.
Lunge risuona un grido: ecco precipita
il tempo, spare con risucchi rapidi
tra i sassi, ogni ricordo è spento; ed io
dall'oscuro mio canto mi protendo
a codesto solare avvenimento.

Voi non pensate ciò che vi rapiva
come oggi, allora, il tacito compagno
che un meriggio lontano vi portava.
Siete voi la mia preda, che m'offrite
un'ora breve di tremore umano.
Perderne non vorrei neppure un attimo:
è questa la mia parte, ogni altra è vana.

Chrysalis

The dark green tree is streaked
with tender yellow and crusted with sap.
The air trembles, all pity for the thirsty
roots, the swelling bark.
These are yours, these scattered
trees, moist, joyous,
revived by April's breath.
For me in this shadow observing you,
another shoot greens again—and you *are*.

Each instant fetches you fresh leaves
and each new tremor of joy is overwhelmed
by your surprise: life in surging waves
whelms this farthest garden corner.
Now your gaze falls to the ground;
your heart, lapped by memories
washing back, almost drowns.
From long ago there comes a cry: and suddenly
years plunge past, disappear, sucked down
among the stones, every memory is snuffed;
and from my dark corner I reach out
toward this advent of light.

You cannot think what it was, then as now,
that ravished your mute companion,
borne here by a noon you never knew.
You are my prey: you offer me
one brief hour of trembling human life.
Not one instant would I lose:
this is my lot, only this has meaning.

La mia ricchezza è questo sbattimento
che vi trapassa e il viso
in alto vi rivolge; questo lento
giro d'occhi che ormai sanno vedere.

Così va la certezza d'un momento
con uno sventolio di tende e di alberi
tra le case; ma l'ombra non dissolve
che vi reclama, opaca. M'apparite
allora, come me, nel limbo squallido
delle monche esistenze; e anche la vostra
rinascita è uno sterile segreto,
un prodigio fallito come tutti
quelli che ci fioriscono d'accanto.

E il flutto che si scopre oltre le sbarre
come ci parla a volte di salvezza;
come può sorgere agile
l'illusione, e sciogliere i suoi fumi.
Vanno a spire sul mare, ora si fondono
sull'orizzonte in foggia di golette.
Spicca una d'esse un volo senza rombo,
l'acque di piombo come alcione profugo
rade. Il sole s'immerge nelle nubi,
l'ora di febbre, trepida, si chiude.
Un glorioso affanno senza strepiti
ci batte in gola: nel meriggio afoso
spunta la barca di salvezza, è giunta:
vedila che sciaborda tra le secche,
esprime un suo burchiello che si volge
al docile frangente—e là ci attende.

Ah crisalide, com'è amara questa
tortura senza nome che ci volve
e ci porta lontani—e poi non restano
neppure le nostre orme sulla polvere;
e noi andremo innanzi senza smuovere
un sasso solo della gran muraglia;
e forse tutto è fisso, tutto è scritto,
e non vedremo sorgere per via

My riches are this agitation
that pervades you, that tilts your face
heavenward, this slow turning
of eyes now able to see.

And so the moment's certainty
dies with a flailing of trees and awnings
between houses; but the shadow
does not dissolve, darkness reclaims you.
And now, with me, you seem to share
this sordid limbo of crippled lives;
and even your rebirth is a barren secret,
a failed miracle like all the others
who flourish at our side.

How clearly the sea beyond the wall
at times speaks of our salvation;
how readily the illusion mounts
the sky, setting its mirages free.
Coiling across the sea, they fuse,
schoonerlike, coasting the horizon.
One soars soundless, skimming
leaden waters like a halcyon
astray. The sun sinks in haze,
the storming hour trembles to a close.
Glorious anticipation throbs breathless
in our throats: in the sultry noon
the sloop of our salvation appears, heaves to
(see the water churning in the shoals!)
then sprouts a boat that rocks
in the gentle swell—and awaits us there.

Ah, chrysalis, this nameless, bitter torrent
overwhelms us and bears us
far away—and in the end leaves nothing,
not even our footprints in the dust;
and we will go doggedly on, never moving
one stone in the great wall;
and perhaps everything is fixed, the script written,
and we will never see, rising on our way,

la libertà, il miracolo,
il fatto che non era necessario!

Nell'onda e nell'azzurro non è scia.
Sono mutati i segni della proda
dianzi raccolta come un dolce grembo.
Il silenzio ci chiude nel suo lembo
e le labbra non s'aprono per dire
il patto ch'io vorrei
stringere col destino: di scontare
la vostra gioia con la mia condanna.
È il voto che mi nasce ancora in petto,
poi finirà ogni moto. Penso allora
alle tacite offerte che sostengono
le case dei viventi; al cuore che abdica
perché rida un fanciullo inconsapevole;
al taglio netto che recide, al rogo
morente che s'avviva
d'un arido paletto, e ferve trepido.

freedom, the miracle,
the unnecessitated act.

No trace of breakthrough in sea or sky.
Along the beach that once sheltered us
in her kindly womb, the signs are changed.
Silence mews us in its shroud
and lips unparted fail to speak
that pact with destiny I would like
to seal: to redeem your joy
with my condemnation.
This is the vow that is born again in me
and afterwards will stir no more. I think then
of those silent sacrifices that sustain
the homes of the living; of the heart that renounces
so a child may laugh, unconscious of the cost;
of the clean cut that slashes through, of the dying
fire that quickens in a withered stalk
and shudders into flame.

Marezzo

Aggotti, e già la barca si sbilancia
e il cristallo dell'acque si smeriglia.
S'è usciti da una grotta a questa rancia
marina che uno zefiro scompiglia.

Non ci turba, come anzi, nell'oscuro,
lo sciame che il crepuscolo sparpaglia,
dei pipistrelli; e il remo che scandaglia
l'ombra non urta più il roccioso muro.

Fuori è il sole: s'arresta
nel suo giro e fiammeggia.
Il cavo cielo se ne illustra ed estua,
vetro che non si scheggia.

Un pescatore da un canotto fila
la sua lenza nella corrente.
Guarda il mondo del fondo che si profila
come sformato da una lente.

Nel guscio esiguo che sciaborda,
abbandonati i remi agli scalmi,
fa che ricordo non ti rimorda
che torbi questi meriggi calmi.

Ci chiudono d'attorno sciami e svoli,
è l'aria un'ala morbida.
Dispaiono: la troppa luce intorbida.
Si struggono i pensieri troppo soli.

Tutto fra poco si farà più ruvido,
fiorirà l'onda di più cupe strisce.

Moiré

You bail, the boat already lists,
and the sea's crystal loses its sheen.
Grotto behind us, we made for this sheet
of bronzed water ruffled by the breeze.

In the half-light the swarming bats
that troubled our arrival have all
gone; oars probing the darkness
no longer strike the rock wall.

Outside, the sun, arrested
in full course, shimmers.
The domed sky shines and burns,
one unbreakable mirror.

A fisherman throws his line
to the current, then
sees the underwater world
deformed, as through a lens.

Water laps the frail shell, oars
trail loose in the oarlocks. Let
memory be still, no remorse
jar this noontime quiet.

Swarms and soarings enfold us,
the air is one soft wing.
They vanish: too much light confounds.
Thoughts too lonely melt away.

Everything will roughen soon,
the waves whiten with darker stripes.

Ora resta così, sotto il diluvio
del sole che finisce.

Un ondulamento sovverte
forme confini resi astratti:
ogni forza decisa già diverte
dal cammino. La vita cresce a scatti.

È come un falò senza fuoco
che si preparava per chiari segni:
in questo lume il nostro si fa fioco,
in questa vampa ardono volti e impegni.

Disciogli il cuore gonfio
nell'aprirsi dell'onda;
come una pietra di zavorra affonda
il tuo nome nell'acque con un tonfo!

Un astrale delirio si disfrena,
un male calmo e lucente.
Forse vedremo l'ora che rasserena
venirci incontro sulla spera ardente.

Digradano su noi pendici
di basse vigne, a piane.
Quivi stornellano spigolatrici
con voci disumane.

Oh la vendemmia estiva,
la stortura nel corso
delle stelle!—e da queste in noi deriva
uno stupore tinto di rimorso.

Parli e non riconosci i tuoi accenti.
La memoria ti appare dilavata.
Sei passata e pur senti
la tua vita consumata.

Ora, che avviene?, tu riprovi il peso
di te, improvvise gravano

Now let everything now stop in place
beneath this flood of fading sun.

A wavering subverts
all forms, contours turn abstract:
all resolve is diverted.
Life grows by fits and starts.

A bonfire without fire, it seems,
a beacon bright with meaning;
in its light our light pales; faces,
commitments burn in its blaze.

Let your brimming heart dissolve
in these waves yawning wider;
let your name splash, sink
like ballast in water.

A solar frenzy mounts,
a malaise, quietly shining.
Now perhaps we'll see the clearing hour
draw near on that burning sphere.

Slopes of lower vineyards
descend upon us, terrace on terrace.
There the gleaners go, singing
with unearthly voices.

Oh, summer harvesting,
a swerve in the courses
of the stars!—and to us
wonder tinted with remorse!

You speak, your own voice is strange.
Memory seems washed away.
You disappear, yet feel your life
absorbed, consumed.

What happens now? You feel your weight
once more, objects that once spun

sui cardini le cose che oscillavano,
e l'incanto è sospeso.

Ah qui restiamo, non siamo diversi.
Immobili così. Nessuno ascolta
la nostra voce più. Così sommersi
in un gorgo d'azzurro che s'infolta.

lie heavy on their pivots
and the spell is broken.

Ah, let's stay here, we're no different.
Motionless, so. Now no one hears
our words. Immersed, like this,
in a blue abyss, that thickens.

Casa sul mare

Il viaggio finisce qui:
nelle cure meschine che dividono
l'anima che non sa più dare un grido.
Ora i minuti sono eguali e fissi
come i giri di ruota della pompa.
Un giro: un salir d'acqua che rimbomba.
Un altro, altr'acqua, a tratti un cigolio.

Il viaggio finisce a questa spiaggia
che tentano gli assidui e lenti flussi.
Nulla disvela se non pigri fumi
la marina che tramano di conche
i soffi leni: ed è raro che appaia
nella bonaccia muta
tra l'isole dell'aria migrabonde
la Corsica dorsuta o la Capraia.

Tu chiedi se così tutto vanisce
in questa poca nebbia di memorie;
se nell'ora che torpe o nel sospiro
del frangente si compie ogni destino.
Vorrei dirti che no, che ti s'appressa
l'ora che passerai di là dal tempo;
forse solo chi vuole s'infinita,
e questo tu potrai, chissà, non io.
Penso che per i più non sia salvezza,
ma taluno sovverta ogni disegno,
passi il varco, qual volle si ritrovi.
Vorrei prima di cedere segnarti
codesta via di fuga
labile come nei sommossi campi
del mare spuma o ruga.
Ti dono anche l'avara mia speranza.

House by the Sea

Here the journey ends:
in these petty cares dividing
a soul no longer able to protest.
Now minutes are implacable, regular
as the flywheel on a pump.
One turn: a rumble of water rushing.
Second turn: more water, occasional creakings.

Here the journey ends, on this shore
probed by slow, assiduous tides.
Only a sluggish haze reveals
the sea woven with troughs
by the mild breezes: hardly ever
in that dead calm
does spiny Corsica or Capraia loom
through islands of migratory air.

You ask: Is this how everything vanishes,
in this thin haze of memories?
Is every destiny fulfilled
in the torpid hour or the breaker's sigh?
I would like to tell you: No. For you
the moment for your passage out of time is near:
transcendence may perhaps be theirs who want it,
and you, who knows, could be one of those. Not I.
There is no salvation, I think, for most,
but every system is subverted by someone, someone
breaks through, becomes what he wanted to be.
Before I yield, let me help you find
such a passage out, a path
fragile as ridge or foam
in the furrowed sea.
And I leave you my hope, too meager

A' nuovi giorni, stanco, non so crescerla:
l'offro in pegno al tuo fato, che ti scampi.

Il cammino finisce a queste prode
che rode la marea col moto alterno.
Il tuo cuore vicino che non m'ode
salpa già forse per l'eterno.

for my failing strength to foster
in days to come. I offer it
to you, my pledge to your fate, that you
break free.

My journey ends on these shores
eroded by the to-and-fro of the tides.
Your heedless heart, so near, may even now
be lifting sail for the eternities.

I morti

Il mare che si frange sull'opposta
riva vi leva un nembo che spumeggia
finché la piana lo riassorbe. Quivi
gettammo un dì su la ferrigna costa,
ansante più del pelago la nostra
speranza!—e il gorgo sterile verdeggia
come ai dì che ci videro fra i vivi.

Or che aquilone spiana il groppo torbido
delle salse correnti e le rivolge
d'onde trassero, attorno alcuno appende
ai rami cedui reti dilunganti
sul viale che discende
oltre lo sguardo;
reti stinte che asciuga il tocco tardo
e freddo della luce; e sopra queste
denso il cristallo dell'azzurro palpebra
e precipita a un arco d'orizzonte
flagellato.
                        Più d'alga che trascini
il ribollio che a noi si scopre, muove
tale sosta la nostra vita: turbina
quanto in noi rassegnato a' suoi confini
risté un giorno; tra i fili che congiungono
un ramo all'altro si dibatte il cuore
come la gallinella
di mare che s'insacca tra le maglie;
e immobili e vaganti ci ritiene
una fissità gelida.
                        Così
forse anche ai morti è tolto ogni riposo
nelle zolle: una forza indi li tragge
spietata più del vivere, ed attorno,

The Dead

The sea crashing against the opposing
shore lifts a cloud that spumes
till reabsorbed by the shoals. Here one day,
against this iron coast, we hurled our hope
higher than the heaving sea,
and the barren abyss turns green again
as once in days that saw us
still here among the living.

Now that the north wind smooths the raging knot
of brackish currents, driving them back
where they began, someone has hung his nets
on the slashed boughs, draping
the path that sinks down
out of sight—
bleached nets drying in the late cold
touch of the light, while overhead
the blue crystal of the sky blinks
and plunges to an arc of storm-lashed
horizon.
          More than seaweed dragged
by the boiling now revealed, our life stirs
against such torpor: whatever in us
was resigned to limit, by one day stilled,
now seethes; between the strands weaving
branch to branch, the heart thrashes
like the gallinule
trapped in the meshes
where an icy stasis holds us fast,
motionless, migratory.
                    So too perhaps
even the dead in the ground may be denied
all repose: a force more pitiless

larve rimorse dai ricordi umani,
li volge fino a queste spiagge, fiati
senza materia o voce
traditi dalla tenebra; ed i mozzi
loro voli ci sfiorano pur ora
da noi divisi appena e nel crivello
del mare si sommergono . . .

than life pulls them thence, from all around
driving them toward this coast—ghosts
tortured by human memories, breaths
without voice or substance, betrayed
by darkness; and even now their thwarted flights,
so close to us still, brush by,
then drift down in the sea
that sifts them. . . .

Delta

La vita che si rompe nei travasi
secreti a te ho legata:
quella che si dibatte in sé e par quasi
non ti sappia, presenza soffocata.

Quando il tempo s'ingorga alle sue dighe
la tua vicenda accordi alla sua immensa,
ed affiori, memoria, più palese
dall'oscura regione ove scendevi,
come ora, al dopopioggia, si riaddensa
il verde ai rami, ai muri il cinabrese.

Tutto ignoro di te fuor del messaggio
muto che mi sostenta sulla via:
se forma esisti o ubbia nella fumea
d'un sogno t'alimenta
la riviera che infebbra, torba, e scroscia
incontro alla marea.

Nulla di te nel vacillar dell'ore
bige o squarciate da un vampo di solfo
fuori che il fischio del rimorchiatore
che dalle brume approda al golfo.

Delta

That life breaking off, secretly transfusing
mine, I have bound to you: of you,
your stifled presence, that conflicted life
seems almost unaware.

When Time backs up behind its weir,
you adjust your days to that vast flood;
and, brighter than before, memory manifest,
you rise from that dark world where you descended,
as now, after rain, the green of the trees
intensifies, on walls the cinnabar.

I know nothing of you, only your speechless
message that sustains me on my way. Whatever
you are, phantasma or vision in the blur
of a dream, the force that feeds you
is the seething of this feverish torrent
crashing against the tide.

No sign of you in the flickering hours
of gray fog cleft by flares of sulphur.
Only the whistle of the tug looming
from the fog, making for shore.

Incontro

Tu non m'abbandonare mia tristezza
sulla strada
che urta il vento forano
co' suoi vortici caldi, e spare; cara
tristezza al soffio che si estenua: e a questo,
sospinta sulla rada
dove l'ultime voci il giorno esala
viaggia una nebbia, alta si flette un'ala
di cormorano.

La foce è allato del torrente, sterile
d'acque, vivo di pietre e di calcine;
ma più foce di umani atti consunti,
d'impallidite vite tramontanti
oltre il confine
che a cerchio ci rinchiude: visi emunti,
mani scarne, cavalli in fila, ruote
stridule: vite no: vegetazioni
dell'altro mare che sovrasta il flutto.

Si va sulla carraia di rappresa
mota senza uno scarto,
simili ad incappati di corteo,
sotto la volta infranta ch'è discesa
quasi a specchio delle vetrine,
in un'aura che avvolge i nostri passi
fitta e uguaglia i sargassi
umani fluttuanti alle cortine
dei bambù mormoranti.

Se mi lasci anche tu, tristezza, solo
presagio vivo in questo nembo, sembra
che attorno mi si effonda

Encounter

Stay, my sorrow, do not
desert me on this road lashed by eddying
scirocco winds, flailing, then
dying; sorrow, dear
to the dying breeze
on which, lifting over the anchorage
where day now breathes its final voices,
floats a cloud, tilting skyward
a cormorant wing.

Where the river meets the sea, its mouth
is arid waste, alive with limewash and stony rubbish—
but more a sluice for the trash
of human acts, of wan, twilit lives setting
beyond the horizon
whose circle walls us in: emaciated faces,
bony hands, horses filing past, screeching
wheels—not lives, no, but vegetation
of the other sea that straddles this.

We move along a rutted road, caked
mud, grooved, undeviating,
like a hooded cortège crawling
under a weary sky lowering now
almost to window level, in air
so dense it tangles our steps,
and this human seaweed writhes
and sways in the breeze like curtains
of whispering bamboo.

If you leave me, my sorrow,
sole living portent in this swarm,
a sound seems to diffuse

un ronzio qual di sfere quando un'ora
sta per scoccare;
e cado inerte nell'attesa spenta
di chi non sa temere
su questa proda che ha sorpresa l'onda
lenta, che non appare.

Forse riavrò un aspetto: nella luce
radente un moto mi conduce accanto
a una misera fronda che in un vaso
s'alleva s'una porta di osteria.
A lei tendo la mano, e farsi mia
un'altra vita sento, ingombro d'una
forma che mi fu tolta; e quasi anelli
alle dita non foglie mi si attorcono
ma capelli.

Poi più nulla. Oh sommersa!: tu dispari
qual sei venuta, e nulla so di te.
La tua vita è ancor tua: tra i guizzi rari
dal giorno sparsa già. Prega per me
allora ch'io discenda altro cammino
che una via di città,
nell'aria persa, innanzi al brulichio
dei vivi; ch'io ti senta accanto; ch'io
scenda senza viltà.

around me like the chirr of the hands
before the striking of the clock,
and I slump, unmoving, in the hopeless
wait for someone ignorant of fear
here on this shore surprised by the sluggish
tide—who does not appear.

I may regain a face: in the glancing
light, impulse draws me
to a spindly plant raised
in a pot by a tavern door.
Toward it I reach a hand and feel, fusing
with mine, another life that bears the one form
torn from me; and, like rings
on my fingers, not leaves, but hair
curls around me.

Then nothing more. O drowned presence, you disappear
as you came, and I know nothing of you.
Your life is yours still, dispersed now
in the fitful glintings of day. Pray for me then,
pray that I descend by some other road
than a city street,
in the violet air, against the teeming tide
of the living, that I sense you at my side,
that I go down,
unflinching.

Seacoasts

Riviere,
bastano pochi stocchi d'erbaspada
penduli da un ciglione
sul delirio del mare;
o due camelie pallide
nei giardini deserti,
e un eucalipto biondo che si tuffi
tra sfrusci e pazzi voli
nella luce;
ed ecco che in un attimo
invisibili fili a me si asserpano,
farfalla in una ragna
di fremiti d'olivi, di sguardi di girasoli.

Dolce cattività, oggi, riviere
di chi s'arrende per poco
come a rivivere un antico giuoco
non mai dimenticato.
Rammento l'acre filtro che porgeste
allo smarrito adolescente, o rive:
nelle chiare mattine si fondevano
dorsi di colli e cielo; sulla rena
dei lidi era un risucchio ampio, un eguale
fremer di vite,
una febbre del mondo; ed ogni cosa
in se stessa pareva consumarsi.

Oh allora sballottati
come l'osso di seppia dalle ondate
svanire a poco a poco;
diventare
un albero rugoso od una pietra
levigata dal mare; nei colori

Seacoasts,
a few spears of sawgrass
waving from a cliff
above the frenzy of the sea will do;
or two faded camellias
in deserted gardens,
and a golden eucalyptus plunging
among rustlings and birds crazily bursting
toward the light:
and instantly
unseen threads entwine me, butterfly
netted in a web
of quivering olives, sunflower eyes.

Sweet captivity, today, of these coasts
for the man who yields, briefly succumbing,
as though reliving an old
never to be forgotten game.
O seacoasts, what a tang was in that drink
you gave to one bewildered adolescent boy:
humpbacked hills fusing with the sky
of bright blue mornings; in sand
along the beaches, the undertow ran strong
but no stronger than that shiver of being alive
in a world on fire; and everything seemed consumed
by its own inward blazing.

Days of tumbling and tossing
like cuttlefish bones in the breakers,
vanishing bit by bit;
becoming
gnarled tree or sea-polished
pebble; melting away

fondersi dei tramonti; sparir carne`
per spicciare sorgente ebbra di sole,
dal sole divorata . . .
                    Erano questi,
riviere, i voti del fanciullo antico
che accanto ad una rósa balaustrata
lentamente moriva sorridendo.

Quanto, marine, queste fredde luci
parlano a chi straziato vi fuggiva.
Lame d'acqua scoprentisi tra varchi
di labili ramure; rocce brune
tra spumeggi; frecciare di rondoni
vagabondi . . .
                    Ah, potevo
credervi un giorno o terre,
bellezze funerarie, auree cornici
all'agonia d'ogni essere.
                    Oggi torno
a voi più forte, o è inganno, ben che il cuore
par sciogliersi in ricordi lieti—e atroci.
Triste anima passata
e tu volontà nuova che mi chiami,
tempo è forse d'unirvi
in un porto sereno di saggezza.
Ed un giorno sarà ancora l'invito
di voci d'oro, di lusinghe audaci,
anima mia non più divisa. Pensa:
cangiare in inno l'elegia; rifarsi;
non mancar più.
                    Potere
simili a questi rami
ieri scarniti e nudi ed oggi pieni
di fremiti e di linfe,
sentire
noi pur domani tra i profumi e i venti
un riaffluir di sogni, un urger folle
di voci verso un esito; e nel sole
che v'investe, riviere,
rifiorire!

in sunset colors, to dissolve as flesh
and flow back, a spring drunk on sunlight,
devoured by sunlight. . . .
                              O seacoasts,
this was his prayer, that boy I used to be,
standing by a rusty balustrade,
who died slowly, smiling.

How much, O seas, these cold lights
speak to that tormented soul who fled you!
Broadswords of water disclosed through fissures
in swaying branches; brown rocks
in the spume; arrow-flash of roving
martins. . . .
                    Ah, seacoasts, if only someday
I could believe in you again,
funereal beauties, framing in gold
the agony of every being.
                              Today I come home to you
a stronger man (or I deceive myself), although
my heart almost melts in memories, happy
but also bitter. Sad soul of my past,
and you, fresh purpose summoning me now,
perhaps the time has come to moor you
in some harbor, more calm, more wise.
And someday, once again, golden voices, bold
illusions will summon me forth
a soul no longer divided. Think:
change elegy to hymn; make yourself new;
lack no more—
                    If only,
like these branches
yesterday bare and sere, bursting now
with sap and quiverings,
I could feel—
even I, tomorrow, among fragrances and winds—
fresh-running dreams, a wild rush of voices
surging toward an outlet; and in the sunlight
that swathes you, seacoasts,
flower anew!

Notes and Commentary

The following notes are based in part upon Montale's own comments (all too sparse, alas, where *Cuttlefish Bones* is concerned). Like every present and future translator of Montale, I am indebted to Rosanna Bettarini and Gianfranco Contini, the editors of M.'s complete poetic works, *Eugenio Montale / L'opera in versi* (Turin, 1980), which contains both variant drafts and M.'s notes to successive editions of the book as well as relevant correspondence, interviews, and essays. I have also cited passages bearing on M.'s individual and general poetic practice from the poet's critical essays, principally those gathered in *Sulla poesia* (Milan, 1976).

Interpretative studies of M.'s poetry have proliferated in recent years, not only in Italy but throughout Europe and America. No serious translator of the poetry can perform his task without consulting the better Italian critics, above all D'Arco Silvio Avalle, Gianfranco Contini, Marco Forti, Angelo Jacomuzzi, Silvio Ramat, Gilberto Lonardi, Romano Luperini, Vincenzo Mengaldo, Sergio Solmi, and Alvaro Valentini. And in the last decade a number of perceptive studies of M. have appeared in America and Britain. These have the merit of drawing upon the best Italian work and qualifying it significantly by the inevitable shift of national and critical focus, and are readily accessible to the reader without Italian. Those on whom I have relied most heavily, and whose work I have cited most frequently, even when I disagree, include:

Almansi, Guido, and Merry, Bruce. *Eugenio Montale / The Private Language of Poetry*. Edinburgh, Scotland, 1977.

Cambon, Glauco. *Eugenio Montale's Poetry / A Dream in Reason's Presence*. Princeton, N.J., 1982.

Cary, Joseph. *Three Modern Italian Poets / Saba, Ungaretti, Montale*. New York, N.Y., 1969; 2d edition, revised and enlarged, Chicago, 1993.

Huffman, Claire de C. L. *Montale and the Occasions of Poetry*. Princeton, N.J., 1983.

West, Rebecca J. *Eugenio Montale / Poet on the Edge*. Cambridge, Mass., 1981.

I am also indebted to M.'s French translator, Patrice Angelini (Eugenio Montale, *Poésies I, Os de Seiche,* Paris, 1966). Even while I often differ in interpretation of details (inevitable when dealing with a poet as difficult and elusive as M.), Angelini's attentive concern for the poet's meaning provided a check against the mind-sets that often bedevil translators.

My notes are not systematic, nor, despite their length, do they aim at comprehensiveness. M.'s poetry is too intricately woven, too elliptical and prosodically inflected, to sanction the effort. My aim has been to supply factual material helpful to reading, or not misreading, the poems; to indicate the dates of individual poems in a book whose order is not chronological but thematic; and, finally, to provide the interpretative commentary that a reader coming to M.'s poetry for the first or even second time might find useful. Ideally, the making of commentaries, like translations, should be a cooperative, not competitive enterprise. If the commentary of others cannot be significantly bettered, then it deserves to be cited, not raided and rephrased. I have accordingly included commentary, often of considerable length, by those critics who in my judgment best mediated the poems and from whom I learned the most. Extensive exegesis has been reserved for poems that seemed exceptionally important in their own right or that illuminated a particular aspect of M.'s poetry. In those cases where existing commentary seemed inadequate or perfunctory, I have offered my own; occasionally, for the sake of clarity, I have added my own initials. Finally, in order to avoid confusion, I have ventured, except in cases of interpretative disagreement, to intrude my own translations of M.'s poetry into the commentators' texts. M.'s own notes and self-commentary have been indicated throughout by the use of the initials *E.M.* at the beginning of the entry. In a few cases I have supplemented critiques by others with brief commentaries of my own, marked by triple asterisks.

IN LIMINE (1924)

In limine (Lat.) = at the threshold.

E.M.: "It had to be either *summa* or the *envoi* of all the rest [of the book]."

In a letter to Giacinto Spagnoletti (August 27, 1960):

> It's a bit difficult for me to manage working at the present; my genre is wholly a waiting for the miracle, and in this day and age, with no religion, miracles are very rarely sighted. Once the book *[Ossi di seppia]* is done—and it might be said that it's almost done—I'll either alter the visual element, changing my genre, or silentium. I've no desire for further self-vivisection. But, "Rejoice, this breeze . . ." exists and . . . has been witnessed with strong feeling. Now all that's left me are bits of a certain "chrysalis" that, some day or other, will emerge. . . .

Rebecca J. West (12–18) provides perceptive reading of this poem and its function as thematic *envoi*—or perhaps *summa*—to the book as a whole:

> In this first collection Montale seeks to create a unique poetic space, to forge a voice and to confront the inevitable questions implicitly asked of all poets. What is poetry in general and this poetry in particular about? What does this poetry open out to the readers in experiential and epistemological terms? How might the reader best orient himself to and establish contact with this poetic vision? I am not suggesting that these concerns were completely or even partially conscious ones for Montale, for as he later wrote concerning the creation of his first voice: "I obeyed a need of musical expression. I wanted my word to be more adherent than that of other poets whom I had known. . . . And my desire for adherence remained musical, instinctive, unprogrammatic." This desire for adherence resulted first in the toning down of the poetic voice. As Gianfranco Contini, one of the earliest and most perceptive of Montale's readers, noted, "Montale's discourse is a discourse with a 'familiar' tone and timbre, a subdued, 'domestic' voice that presupposes, moreover, [the presence of] a very close interlocutor." He refers, of course, to the well-known *tu,* or informal "you," of Montale's poetic dialogues, of which the poet wrote many years after its initial appearance in *"In*

limine," "*I critici ripeteno, / da me depistati, / che il mio tu è un istituto* (the critics repeat, / by me put off the track, / that my *you* is an institution),*" thus effectively precluding any further such critical pronouncements. Institution or not, the imagined interlocutor is one of the lexical and psychological constants of Montale's poetry. It determines to a great extent the intimate and even conversational quality of much of the poetry as well as the sense of direct communicative thrust, as the reader feels himself to be personally addressed, called to, warned, and counseled by the informal imperative form in which the *tu* is most often contained.

"*In limine*" opens with just such an address—*Godi* (Enjoy)—followed by a crescendo of imperatives in the final stanza—*cerca* (seek), *balza fuori* (jump out); *fuggi* (flee), *va* (go). These imperatives tell us to enjoy, but we are also warned to flee, to go away from the space created in the poem. Thus, as Almansi and Merry so incisively point out, "the '*tu*' is the reader himself who has to find a way out from the white space at the end of the poem. The adventure begins in the types that form the printed composition, but the final solution lies beyond them." Of course, the *tu* is also and perhaps primarily a dramatic presence in the poem, the "other" for whom escape is urged. But if we read the poem as a poem about poetry's emergence as well as about experience that is beyond literature, then it is accurate to call it "a self-questioning poem" conscious of its own status as poem and implicitly confronting the questions of its relationship with the reader.

In order to pursue this self-questioning it is first helpful to describe the immediate or literal dramatic situation created in "*In limine.*" The first-person speaker, enclosed in a static garden *(pomario)* filled with "a dead / tangle of memories" *(un morto / viluppo di memorie),* is touched by the stirrings of wind and change he senses outside the garden walls. Unable, however, to escape these boundaries, he urges that the other, who is not named or specified in any way, attempt salvation by getting beyond the walls, while he will stay behind, confronted by the thought of her breakthrough. The poem can bear a less literal reading, however. Where, in fact, is the *I* of the poem speaking from? The wind enters into a garden, called variously *pomario, orto,* and *lembo di terra* (orchard, vegetable garden, strip of earth). It is also called *reliquiario* (reliquary) and then *crogiuolo* (crucible). This is a space not untouched by extraliteral associations; it is soon recognizable as a literary garden not only because the *topos* inevitably comes to mind but because the poet himself invests it with multiple transforming and transformed identities: garden to reliquary to crucible. Although the word *orto* will ultimately take on particular symbolic resonance in Montale's poetry (it is one of the lexical leitmotifs of *Ossi*), it is more fruitful in this instance to consider further the words *pomario* and *lembo*.

One Italian critic of Montale has suggested that there is "a strict affinity between *pomario* and *pomerium (pomerio)* and between *lembo* and *limbo*." This affinity is etymologically determined: the first two words refer to spaces behind or near walls, the second two to edges or borders. . . . *Pomerium* is the Latin term designating . . . a consecrated space, usually running along both the inside and outside of the city walls, which had to be left free of buildings; it was, in short, a marginal space or edge that belonged neither to the undefined area outside of it nor to the daily life of the city within but that allowed for the delineation of the concepts of in and out, profane and sacred, structured and wild. Similarly, *limbo* is that space designated for those neither fully damned nor fully beatified, as in-between space in Dante's *Commedia* is the place of *"gente di molto valore"* (people of great esteem), specifically the poets, among them Vergil, Homer, Horace, Ovid, and Lucan. This limbo is *cerchiato d'alte mura* (surrounded by high walls) in Dante's portrayal, much as Montale's *lembo di terra* is surrounded by an *erto muro* (steep wall). . . .

If we accept that the garden in which the speaker is dramatically placed is . . . poetry itself, we see that this space is not untouched by temporal concerns. That is, it is not some fixed garden of pure aesthetic delights entirely divorced from time but rather a space that is transformed *(si trasforma)* from reliquary to crucible, from the static coldness of a container of dead relics to the seething heat of a melting pot, the container of potential new forms. The reliquary is clearly linked to the past in that it holds "a dead / tangle of memories" and "the stories, the acts / canceled out by the game of the future." The term *reliquiario* is again used many years after the writing of this poem in Montale's short story entitled *"Reliquie"* (Relics) to describe "a box where [were kept] newspaper clippings, old letters tied up with a ribbon, and some little saints that [he dared not] destroy. . . ." These are lifeless objects representing once living and lived moments; they are, in short, tangible memories, memories being the most private form of history. They remain lifeless and useless unless brought back to some new form of life. Montale's raw material for his future poetry will in great part be these relics, or personal memories, transformed and suscitated through poetic creation. . . .

It is . . . clear from this first poem that Montale assigns no revelatory or salutary function to poetry. The other is urged to seek the phantom who might save her somewhere outside the confines of the garden. The edge is a dangerous place to be; it holds out no certainties and offers minimal comforts to the one poised on it—*ora la sete / mi sara lieve, meno acre la ruggine* . . . (now thirst / will be mild for me, less sharp the rust . . .). What is implicit in this poem will become explicit in succeeding poems: to be in an edge-space is to accept fully the ambiguities, the double-edged uncertainties of such a position. What is here suggested as a general attitude toward poetry later becomes the very stuff of which Montale's poetry is made, thematically, stylistically, and philosophically. . . .

Limits, edges, margins—all are central to Montale's poetic imagination and to his evolving poetics, their importance is most clearly evident in *Ossi di seppia,* where the poet is involved in the creation of his first voice. The origins of this tendency to stay on the edges, to mute the poetic voice, to emphasize the concept of eccentricity, may have been primarily psychological . . . or perhaps cultural and historical . . . or most likely some combination of these and other factors. Whatever the source . . . it is from the very first imbued with a sense of the limitations of poetic discourse understood not as the full lyric expression of captured truths expressed in a confident or prophetic voice but rather as the necessarily counter-eloquent and understated search for its own possible meaning. Poetry is "more a means of knowledge than of representation," a process, a "realm of pure possibility. . . ." Montale identified his primary *motivi* (motives and motifs) as three: *il paesaggio* (the landscape), *l'amore* (love), and *l'evasione* (evasion, escape). These moving forces behind the poetry and its major thematic centers can be seen to capture in various ways the inter-structurability characteristic of the marginal, the betwixt and between status attributable both to the dramatic situations portrayed in these early poems and to the very concept of the art of poetry that they imply. . . .

For another rewardingly sensitive analysis of this important poem and of M.'s poetics in general, see Claire de C. L. Huffman, "Montale for the English-Speaking: The Case of '*In limine*,' " *Forum Italicum*, XXIII, 1–2 (Spring–Fall 1989).

The Lemon Trees (1922)

With the possible exception of "The Eel" and *"Bring me the sunflower . . . ,"* this poem is probably M.'s best known and most admired. It is also a genuine manifesto, the poet's announcement of his break with the Mandarin conventions dominant in Italian poetry of the time. The late Glauco Cambon, one of M.'s most astute interpreters, comments (8–11):

> "The Lemon Trees" is a poem amounting to a personal manifesto at the very outset of the book after the epigraph-like piece *"In limine"*; it proclaims the rejection of stale literary convention in favor of a rediscovery of humble, unadulterated reality and language, fusing the quest for beauty with the quest for truth:
>
> > *il filo da disbrogliare che finalmente ci metta
> > nel mezzo di una veritá*
>
> [the thread that, disentangled, might at last lead us / to the center of a truth]
>
> and it caps these sober statements with the hymning finale heralded by the "golden trumpets of sunni-ness"—as strong an affirmation of life as one could ever expect from the bemused author and doubting-Thomas persona of *Ossi di seppia*. The relaxed conversational utterance, the liberal admixture of free verse with regular lines of amply varying length, and the anti-grandiose focus, a clear inheritance from the so-called Crepuscular poets who ever since the start of the new century had waged a quiet battle against highfalutin' vatic style in verse, might deceive the unwary reader

about the real scope of this discreet *ars poetica*. Rhythmic suppleness, tonal modulation, verbal precision are its secret; and the care that went into its making also shows from the variants exhibited in the modern manuscript collection of Pavia University, where a few lexical alternatives are weighed or adopted while an entire stanza, the capitally important third one of the four that have always made up the poem from its first publication . . . at one point had been crossed out in the autograph manuscript to be later recast, with some changes, on the back of the same sheet, right after the text of stanza 4. The importance of the recent stanza comes from its being the epistemologically oriented one among its three companion units, which rely on thematics, mood, and scene (with a glance at the stylistic implications of the pertinent choices). Stanzas 1 and 2 outline a literary policy in the very act of describing a locale where "we the poor can have our part of riches . . . , / the smell of lemons." Stanza 4 celebrates the victory of spring over winter, of light and color over grayness, of joy over urban tedium, applauding the reward of fidelity to the unadorned truth of simple things. But stanza 3 (and this must have been the reason for the poet's doubt and temporary rejection) goes far beyond that impressionistic approach to probe a further dimension, a clearly intellectual one. "In these silences . . . things / let themselves go and seem on the verge / of betraying their ultimate secret"; and characteristically for Montale, that secret is a matter of discovering "a mistake of Nature, / the dead point of the world, the ring [in the Chain of Being] that does not hold."

Thus while the metaphysical truth he seeks can only be glimpsed and not possessed, negatively formulated and not embalmed in foolproof arguments, it becomes for that very reason the magnet of Montale's poetics—a cognitively oriented kind of poetics from the start, sharply separated from aesthetic hedonism however keen its sensuous organs. *"Lo sguardo fruga d'intorno, / le mente indaga accorda disunisce* (Eyesight searches everything around, / mind investigates harmonizes disjoins)": the act of aesthetic perception is one and the same thing with the heuristic process of knowledge, and the very sequence of verbs is significant here, causal though it may sound at first. The eye functions from the start as a cognitive organ; it "searches" *(fruga)* instead of merely "taking things in." The mind develops that cue on a more abstract level, analysis following sensuous prehension and detached "investigation" superseding the sense-bound, almost tactilely qualified action of "searching." The naive unity of sensuous perception breaks down into different acts of phases, which are not necessarily irreversible: after (or simultaneous with) investigation comes "harmonizing" *(accorda)* and its contrary, *"disjoining" (disunisce)*. . . .

Standard philosophical terminology (especially of the Idealist type prevailing when this poem was written) . . . would speak of analysis and synthesis as the two essential operations of speculative intellect, synthesis inevitably superseding analysis. But . . . at this point, the Montalean elf—a learned elf at that—shows his mettle and subverts the established harmony. *Disunisce* (disjoins) is the conclusive word in the sequence. Taking apart what has been conventionally joined in language, criticizing the stereotypes of intellectual currency is germane to the skeptic vein in Montale's thinking, and in this particular context, where one would least expect it, that cleansing operation "in the expanding aroma" (of lemons at twilight) sets the stage for a visionary moment that makes sense of the previous negations:

> *Sono i silenzi in cui si vede*
> *in ogni ombra umana che si allontana*
> *qualche disturbata Divinità.*

[These are the silences in which one sees / in each departing human shade / some disturbed Divinity.]

The phonic and semantic link between *disunisce* (disjoins) and *disturbata* (disturbed) serves to precipitate a final resolution of meaning in *Divinità,* epiphany aided by alliteration. Its radiance will extend to the symmetrically conclusive word *solarità* (sunniness) of the following and last stanza by way of distant rhyme. The two preceding stanzas ended on the word *limoni* (lemons), an identical rhyme well attuned to the happily literal drift of the first half of the poem: it's as if the rhyme said, just by being there, that lemons are lemons and nothing else, nor do they need to be anything else, for their significance is in their reality, in their presence. By contrast, the *Divinità-solarità* rhyme of the two last stanzas introduces a semantic swerve into the unpredictable; even if it is "illusion" (as the first line of stanza 4 says), the epiphany favored by twilight's silence and lemon aroma, which activate the mind in a contemplative direction, suspending the quotidian, will have given us a spiritual break, and we shall then be able to recognize the fullness of reality *(solarità)* without having recourse to mere "shadows."

For additional commentary, see Cary, 251–54.

★　★　★

W.A.: *and trumpets of gold pour forth / epiphanies of Light.* Literally translated, the Italian reads, "golden trumpets of *'solarità'* [sunniness] / pelt us with their songs." The problem is adequate rendering of that final, emphatic *solarità,* which corresponds to the capitalized *Divinità* that closes the previous stanza. "Sunniness" seems lexically and prosodically unacceptable. As for "solarity," it is, alas, not an English word at all, and to close with a neologism would, I thought, be a mistake. Both word and line needed to be rethought in terms of M.'s putative poetic strategy. In the poem's opening lines, M. rejects the formal gardens of the "laureled poets" (i.e., D'Annunzio above all, but also D'Annunzians, classicizing "Parnassians," and others) for the humbler pathway that leads to the lemon grove. The poem itself is a journey along the arduous poetic path that, followed to the end by the patiently searching imagination, at last comes upon the triumphant springtime miracle of the lemon trees, that is, upon a poetics of immanence and incarnation: an ordinary world of real objects animated by an indwelling divinity. D'Annunzio and the literary Parnassians, M. suggests, employ lofty Greek and Latinate abstractions without having won the right to them; their abstractions have been removed from their component particulars. Implicitly but unmistakably, by right of humility, persistence, and imaginative toil, M. claims to have *earned* the right to his closing abstraction, *solarità.* That "epiphanies of light" inadequately renders the explosive precision of the Italian will be apparent—an attempt (failed, no doubt, since commentary seems required) to do justice to the semantic demands of the poem by introducing with "epiphany" the *process of abstraction* implicit in M.'s *solarità.* Moreover, "epiphany" in its Italian form *(epifania)* had been introduced into Italian poetry and repeatedly employed by none other than D'Annunzio, whose poetics are subtly but unmistakably taken to task by M.'s poem.

English Horn (1916–20)

Published, along with "Seacoasts," in a group of poems entitled *"Accordi (Sensi e fantasmi di una adolescente)"* ["Chords (Sensations and Fancies of an Adolescent Girl)"], in the journal *Primo Tempo* in 1922. The original group consisted of six poems: "Violins," "Cellos," "Flutes, Bassoons," "Oboe," "English Horn," "Brasses," a suite based upon the moody daydreamings and emotional velleities of an unnamed adolescent girl as she "experiences" the various instruments.

M. wrote to Giacinto Spagnoletti in 1960 [see Spagnoletti, "Preistoria di Montale," in Silvio Ramat, ed., *Omaggio a Montale* (Milan, 1966), 121–22] as follows:

> I couldn't assign a date to "Chords" with absolute precision: it certainly followed the first real and proper *osso ["To laze at noon . . ."]* but is much earlier than "Seacoasts" (March, 1920), the poem that recapitulated my juvenilia, and which I inserted into the *Ossi,* even though it's uncomfortable there (it's a synthesis written before the analysis!). "English Horn" was the only poem in the series that could be detached. What displeased me, and still displeases me, in the series is the general sense as well as the naive pretense of imitating musical instruments (apart from the filler to be found here and there). So I have to conclude that in my youthful *château d' eaux* (as Lorenzo Montanto defines my poetry), alongside a more troubled vein—or even *within* that vein—the leaner but more limpid vein of poetry had been making headway for quite awhile. So the whole opening section of the *Ossi* (except for *"In limine,"* a poem strangely misunderstood by my anthologists) belongs to proto-Montale, and included in this group—though even within such limits later rejected by me—are the poems of "Chords."

Falsetto (1924)

The poem was originally dedicated to "E.R." [Esterina Rossi], who inspired it. Eighteen years old in the summer of 1924, she fascinated the shy young M. with her beauty and the grace of her diving at the beach of Genova Quarto.

Cary's exegesis (243–46) of this deservedly famous poem provides insight into M.'s themes and structural techniques at the time:

> The poem is ultimately a meditation on "life" but the meditation is presented dramatically. The speaker is not young: he contemplates youth in the person of Esterina, "menaced"—as he puts it in the first line—by her twenty years. The scene is on the riviera. There is sun, a shore or *lido,* a flat rock glittering with salt, a diving board and—bounding and defining everything—the sea. And there is Esterina whom the observer sees enveloped in the ambivalent "grey-pink cloud" of her young age:
>
> > Salgono i venti autunni,
> > t' avviluppano andate primavere. . . .
>
> [Your twenty autumns mount, / springtimes past enfold you. . . .]
>
> In the first stanza she emerges phoenixlike in triumph out of the progressively more sinister cloud metamorphosed first into hellish and windtossed smokiness, then into a *fiotto di cenere* (wave or breaker of ashes). She rises "scorched" (by the sun? by the crowding, cannibalistic, infernal years?— the ambiguity is intended and is pertinent both thematically and dramatically) and, bathed in an atmosphere compounded of the speaker's knowledgeable premonitions and her own "tragic" innocence, is lyrically transfigured:
>
> > . . . proteso a un' avventura più lontana
> > l' intento viso che assembra
> > l' arciera Diana.
>
> [. . . stretching toward some new adventure / your face so intense you might be / the huntress Diana.]
>
> With this momentary apotheosis the speaker seems to sense a prophecy sounding for her "in the Elysian spheres" and prays—somewhat against his rueful better knowledge at this point—that it may be "an ineffable concert of little bells" rather than the dull *toc* of a "cracked jug struck."
>
> Stanza two develops the lines initiated previously . . . but modifies her "divinity" in more naturalistic and ele-

mental terms. Here Esterina has been allied with the natural forces that menaced in stanza one. Amphibian, a *lido* animal, she stretches her bronzed limbs beneath the sun. The second stanza presents her trustfulness, her "impossible" living in the present (according to *noi,* the grown and wounded who know it untenable) as in itself a force sustained by the sea, that immeasurably more powerful presence that, according to Thales, can create, support, drown and destroy in a pure present unadulterated by harbored memories, principles, anticipations. Montale's sea is something like the blue-fleshed *"Hydra absolue"* of Valéry's *"Cimetière marin"* or the "undinal vast belly" of Crane's *Voyages,* an infinite mass of sheer unperspectived fluidity that looks like joyously utter being from the time- and earthborn human viewpoint. Here, precisely through that innocent improvidence or instinctive trust in higher providence which from that viewpoint "threatens" her, Esterina becomes elect.

The third and two-lined fourth stanzas work out the consequences: the momentary marriage of Esterina and the sea (spark and conflagration, granule of sand and salt and ocean). In the midst of the observer's ruminations she rises from her rock, advances out along the springboard above the Scylla-like "shrieking whirlpool," hesitates "profiled against a ground of pearl," laughs, ". . . and then, as though ravished by a wind, / plunge to the clasping arms / of the god who loves you. / We watch you—we, the race of those / who stick to the shore."

The apotheosis is complete. An absolute distinction has been made between the elect one (who possesses a certain unworldly or "divine" faith not just in self but in the elemental powers surrounding and defining, a total lack of that lacerating sense of contingency and limit which "blocks" and doubtless stamps the features of the observer *pallido e assorto*) and the rest, *noi,* the earthbound, the pacers, *flâneurs* and prisoners whose perfect epithet is Montale's *razza di chi rimane a terra.* This distinction is fundamental not only for "Falsetto" but for a great proportion of the physical-metaphysical world of Montale. That is, the blockade is not absolute: there are those who penetrate it. As we shall see, the recurrent term used to indicate this passage from one state or law of being to another is *il varco:* pass, ford, interstice, gap. The most extraordinary of these creatures who have the secret of *varco* is the *donna* whom Montale comes to call "Clizia" in the pages of his later poetry. Esterina can be seen from our retrospect as one of the harbingers of Clizia, even as Giovanna—*primavera* and *prima verrà*—annunciates Beatrice in the pages of the *Vita nuova*.

A central quality of "Falsetto" . . . is its distinctive timbre or voicing—a unique integration of deep emotion and "worldly" self-ironizing in reaction to that emotion. The title itself provides an example. *Falsetto* means a vocal "falsification" or straining in the uppermost registers primarily for purposes of humor or melodramatic pathos, and the implication for the poem it heralds is that it will be a squeak or bathetic utterance with some pretensions to musicality. Such sarcasm is directed by the speaker at himself, not his subject, and indeed it is the play of his (self-) consciousness occasioned by the sight of Esterina which constitutes the poem's true subject and "action."

A young girl, a tanned and graceful swimmer, rises from the rock where she has been sunning herself and dives into the sea. In other words, very little happens. But she is observed and it is what the observer makes of her which is everything. He sees her, clearly, with much envy, with certain misgivings and some condescension, and with genuine tenderness throughout. He expresses his feelings with a consolidated irony of language, image and tone which does not nullify or in any way diminish them but intensifies and, as it were, profiles them in an atmosphere of self-directed dryness and even mockery. Thus the imagery is fraught with "dialectical" opposition—on the one hand the suave neoclassicism of Esterina's apotheosis (Diana, Elysian spheres, Scyllian whirlpool, the sea as "divine friend," and so on), on the other a naturalistic and local specificity (cracked jug and jingling bells, the lizard and the grass lasso, seaweed, pebbles, etc.). In the same way, certain literary archaisms *(fumea, paventi, assembra, impaura, equorea, lito)* occur throughout the poem and create a sort of phantom and parodic aulicity within the context of its predominantly colloquial language. A similar effect is gained through employing (infrequently) elegant paraphrases in expressing natural objects: thus a springboard becomes *ponticello esiguo* or *tremulo asse* (slender bridgelet, trembling axis), the white-capped water is parnassianly frozen as "ground of pearl." Even the dissonanced rhymes *(nube—chiude, intendi—pav-*

enti, vento—violento, asse—braccia—razze) wink at the "correct" cadences of the poem as a whole.

Minstrels (1923)

E.M.: ". . . when I started writing the first poems of *Cuttle-fish Bones* I had of course some idea of the new music and the new painting. I'd heard Debussy's 'Minstrels,' and in the book's first edition there was a little something that tried to imitate it." ["*Musica sognata* (Dreamed Music)," from "Intentions: Imaginary Interview" in *Sulla poesia* (Milan, 1976), 563]

"Minstrels" is the twelfth and last of Debussy's *Préludes,* I.

POEMS FOR CAMILLO SBARBARO

Camillo Sbarbaro (1886–1967) was an early, close friend of M. as well as a poetic influence. A "literary cousin" of the *crepuscolari* ("Twilight") poets, he also belonged, like Ceccardi, Novaro, and Boine, to a group, not a school, of poets rooted in and drawing upon the landscape of their native Liguria. "Where they came closest to the texture of our soil," M. wrote, "they certainly were a lesson to me." Above all, M. admired "the fidelity and art of Sbarbaro." Eight years older than M., Sbarbaro was closely linked to the "moralist members" of those writers associated with the Crocean journal, *La Voce:* Slataper, Salvemini, and Amendola. The extent of M.'s indebtedness to Sbarbaro can be inferred from the fact that, of the many dedications to friends (Bazlen, Solmi, Cecchi, etc., "to whom these poems owe so much") in early editions of *Ossi di seppia,* only the dedication to Sbarbaro remains. What M. particularly valued in Sbarbaro's life and work was not only the richness and color of his Ligurian landscape, but also a virile, almost tragic resignation, and a noble reticence founded upon a pure-minded innocence earned by honoring "the child within." Technically, M. respected Sbarbaro's concentration and sense of his own limitations, but above all his possession of "a center, a vein of his own" that enabled him "to write entire pages—something very rare these days—which, even if they seem extremely fragmentary, are in fact governed by an emotional consistency." For M.'s own affectionately critical tribute to Sbarbaro, see "Camillo

Sbarbaro" in M., *Sulla poesia* (Milan, 1976), 189–94, and *"Ricordo di Sbarbaro"* (ibid., 335–37). For fuller discussion of Sbarbaro's influence on M.'s poetry, see A. Guerrini, "Montale e Sbarbaro" in *Letture montaliane in occasione dell'80° compleanno del poeta* (Bozzi Editore, Genoa, 1977), 443–52.

1. *Café at Rapallo* (undated)

Adult sophistication and modish worldliness set against the lost innocence of childhood—a persistent Montalean theme. To a fashionable café in worldly Rapallo, frequented by the new (i.e., *arriviste*) Sirens, presumably attracted by the presence of such famous *littérateurs* as Max Beerbohm and, by 1924, expatriates like Pound, M. summons his childlike friend, Sbarbaro. Chronicler of the subtler small passions, a poetic "rememberer," Sbarbaro brings with him another Liguria, an older, greener, but now irrecoverable world. "Often," wrote M. of Sbarbaro:

> the pleasant aspects of nature, the quotidian wonder of the world, his astonished joy at finding himself the living center of this spectacle which death besieges and destroys—all this is enough to keep him afloat on life's phenomena. But at times he feels that all the world's appearances dissolve into smoke and ashes; and that there are cloudy dregs at the bottom of the brimming glass; then a barely restrained sob surfaces, confused memories of paradise lost rise up: but these are lightning flashes in the night. . . . [*Sulla poesia,* 190–91]

★ ★ ★

—*a silver / tinkle: piattini,* literally, "little plates," also means "cymbals." According to M.'s French translator, Angelini, there is an untranslatable pun here on the little silver *(arguti / argento)* cups presented to children at baptism.

—*that greening pasture / where you and I will never graze again:* There is probably a touch of parody here (including M.'s gentle mockery of both himself and Sbarbaro) aimed at the neoclassical manner and motifs of such poets as Cardarelli, also noticeable in "Falsetto" earlier.

2. *Epigram* (undated)

A deft, appreciative, but also fondly critical tribute to Sbarbaro. The epigrammatic homage, like Sbarbaro's best poetry, is itself, appropriately, a "flash," or incandescent image. Sbarbaro, the childlike artisan-poet, transforms his highly colored material into frail but effective form, and consigns his paper boats to the muddy stream (here, as in Eliot, a metaphor for life's turbid reality) where they risk foundering or being swept away. The "kind passing sir" is asked to nudge them safely back to their "cove of pebbles" (the Ligurian seacoast) from which they were launched. Whereas for M., the sea meant—at least much of the time—to be *tempted* by confrontation with the inexplicable rhythms of life and the cosmos, Sbarbaro stuck stubbornly to the security of the coast. He was, as M. observed, "*a man of terra firma. . . .* After leaving Genoa . . . he immediately sequestered himself at Spotorno, facing the sea, which rarely appears in his poems and prose." M. himself, in contrast, is consistently inconsistent, moving, as need drove him, now seaward, now landward. As West (19) observes, "In 'Falsetto' the speaker identifies himself with those *della razza / di chi rimane a terra* ('the race of those / who cling to the shore'), but throughout the entire 'Mediterranean' suite he is a creature of the sea, or at least desirous of such a merging."

Almost a Fantasia (undated)

Cambon (11–12) comments:

> The clearly affirmative note of *"I limoni"* can rise to nearly triumphant pitch in "Almost a Fantasia," where the poetic self envisages a forthcoming spell of its own making that will efface the deadness of daily routine to create a snow-lit fairyland and summon up remembrance of all things past—like a recovered childhood; the "solitary mirth" will find its focus in a "March cockerel" [i.e., 'a hoopoe or two'] alighting on a fence pole. And if . . . the poet's double vision can tilt the scales all the way toward the subjective side and thus momentarily revive the Romantic myth of the poet as wizard, of imagination as a victorious, boundless power, the very first . . . lyric, *"In limine"* . . . sets sharp boundaries to that power and thereby carves out a

"threshold" enclosure for the poet's use as his own locus, while the privilege of breaking away is reserved to others, to the ubiquitous and changeable "you" whom the speaker is addressing. This sense of the limit which sets the authorial persona apart from the fullness of unconfined life marks poem after poem and book after book . . . for boundary lines (between land and sea, between self and reality, between dream and truth, between reason and imagination) are also there to be transgressed, as the "Mediterranean" series shows.

SARCOPHAGI (1923)

E.M. (in a letter to Francesco Messina, September 27, 1924):

> Piero Gobetti has half-pledged to publish my book: in which, dedicated to you, my "Sarcophagi" will appear. The sequence closes with a vision of Life-Death which once again sets the three preceding bas-reliefs, somewhat objective, alongside the rest of my things.

★ ★ ★

A single poem consisting of four movements, each movement except the last devoted to a tableau based upon scenes reminiscent of (and perhaps derived from) real sarcophagi. The iconography, though recognizably classical, is unmistakably Montalean in both details and ensemble. "You" (the reader), addressed as "passerby" according to the convention of classical lament, is strolling through a museum colonnade, guided by the *cicerone*-poet who asks him to pause and meditate on the scenes depicted on the three sarcophagi. In the final poem the reader (merged now it seems with the poet—M.'s "you" and "I," reader and author, like Baudelaire's, repeatedly fuse), evidently feeling that the three tableaux are incomplete, asks the sculptor to provide a fourth, and recommends to him a new (or rather, more ancient) symbolic motif.

The progression of these tableaux is the key to the poem-as-sequence. Failure to take account of sequence here has caused the poem to be written off as a classicizing exercise, though its comparatively late date and M.'s explicit refusal in "The Lemon Trees" to frequent the formal gardens of the "laureled poets" argue against such dismissal. If the tone is elegiacally detached, so too are some of the much admired shorter *Ossi*. What deserves the reader's attentive respect is M.'s knack of engaging Parnassian themes and forms that he then bends to his own poetic purpose. The "passerby" is in fact retracing the familiar classical poetics of death—a gentle Elysian setting in the first tableau; in the second, a mysterious threshold that divides life from death, this world from the underworld; in the third, a benevolent *requiescat* and homage. But in the last poem M. refuses to satisfy the expectation of a fourth tableau and offers instead a rejection of both classical and Christian ways of coping with death. The sculptor is bidden to carve the graves of "those who welcome the embers / of the original flame" with "some sign of peace / light as a toy!" Turning away from the slabs incised with the cross ("the symbol that most disturbs / since in it grief and laughter / are equal, twinned"), he should seek instead

> a frieze so primal
> it knows, remembering, what entices
> the rough soul
> on its road to gracious exile—
> some trifle, a sunflower unfolding
> and rabbits dancing around it. . . .

The sculptor—surely a Montalean poet—must, like his frieze, *remember*. What is remembered is the pagan mystery of joyful rebirth, regeneration earned not by the power of Christ's sufferings on the cross, but simply by virtue of having lived, by accepting with childlike innocence "the embers / of the original flame."

A persistent Montalean theme, this, appropriately capping a poem that anticipates not only later poems in the *Ossi* but some of M.'s most moving meditations on mortality, above all in "Voice That Came with the Coots." If the first three poems are reread from the vantage of the fourth, it is apparent that their Parnassian tableaux have been "seeded" with themes and metaphors central to the entire book. The whole sequence, progressing from death to life, inflects the theme of escape from "blockade" first announced in "The Lemon Trees" and advanced in "Wind and Banners" (the poem that immediately follows "Sarcophagi"). Thus the image of the crackling fire in the third poem is related to the "embers / of the original flame" in the fourth; these in turn are realized in the famous last lines of *"Squander, if you want . . ."*: "I know it well: burning— / this, and only this, is my meaning." Life for M. is a fire; but lived without passion it is death, a death-in-life. Hence, in the first tableau, the passerby is told to continue on his journey because there is "No refuge here for one so dead as you." Not until his "orbit" is completed can he fulfill himself—that is, by his patient persistence, abide his own burning. Until then he lacks the indelible individual features, the achieved *thisness* by which, throughout M.'s work, a man survives extinction. The fire that endures is the volatilization of the "original flame"; the evidence of burning is ashes. "A story [i.e., a destiny] only survives in ashes / persistence is only extinction," M. himself would later declare, affirming the survival of his own poetry in "Little Testament," the penultimate poem of *The Storm and Other Things*.

For M., death is entry into *another order*. That order can be entered only by accepting and enduring "the original flame," or, in a related image, by traveling the road of life to the end. The "passerby" in this sequence of sarcophagi is being urged, by means of the tableaux and the exhortation implied in them, to persist, to go his way, all the way, wherever his road takes him. Only by "moving on" can he enter that other order which the dead—spiritually alive in their sarcophagi—reveal to him. The point is explicit in the later poem, "To My Mother":

> The road ahead
> is not a way; only two hands, a face,
> those hands, that face, the gestures of one
> life that's nothing but itself,
> only this sets you down in that Elysium
> crowded with souls and voices, in which you live. . . .
> *[The Storm and Other Things]*

And of a dead friend, Sergio Fadin, M. would, also later, remark:

> . . . to say that you're no longer here is only to say that you've entered a different order, in that the order in which we loiterers move about, crazy as it is, seems to our way of thinking the only one in which divinity reveals its attributes, is recognized and savored, in the context of a task we don't understand.
>
> ["Visit to Fadin" in *The Storm and Other Things*]

Sarcophagi, in short, are memorials; the poet and his other self, his *semblable,* or "passerby," are, or should be, rememberers. The past in which "dead memories / mesh" (see *"In limine"*) can be revived; through "the stirring of the eternal womb," the "reliquary" becomes "crucible."

Finally, the reader unfamiliar with M.'s œuvre should be aware that the symbolic "sunflower unfolding" recommended to the sculptor in the penultimate line of the fourth poem will be fully realized later in *"Bring me the sunflower . . . ,"* one of M.'s most celebrated lyrics. Later still, it will appear in transmogrified form as Clizia, the Ovidian girl who fell in love with Apollo and was metamorphosed into the heliotrope or sunflower, the divinely redemptive "angel messenger" of M.'s greatest poetry.

OTHER VERSES

Wind and Banners (1925?)

A Ligurian seascape—wind, water, sky—triggers a sudden onslaught of memory. The miraculous "instant of forever"—the remembrance of a woman's figure profiled against the sky—is aroused by a sudden gust that, like memory itself, fastens around the beloved's body, shaping her to its likeness. Her ruffled hair, which the wind had once "tousled" *(scompiglió),* takes form as "an instant's tangle" *(groviglio breve),* a gauzy film—pure ephemerality—fretting a pale *(pallido)* sky. (The image glances back at *"In limine,"* with its "dead memories" sifting into the sea.) It is this tangled mesh, freshening into sudden life ("The world *is* . . ."), that now rises with the wind, spiraling to the hills.

The wind itself is a *sgorgo,* a flood disgorging, pouring forth (whence my "profusion"), placed emphatically at the beginning of the fifth stanza. This brimming overflow is one of M.'s most persistent images of Time, analogous to Plato's "moving image of eternity" or to a Heraclitean torrent ("You can't step into the same river twice") composed of intense, unrepeatable, but also unforgettable "moments." Subsequently the image will be developed in "Delta" ("When Time backs up behind its weir") and "Chrysalis" ("and suddenly / years plunge past, disappear, sucked down / among the stones").

The lifting wind with its changing modalities—gusting, caressing, cradling—and the erotic bittersweetness *(amaro aroma / del mare)* linked to the salt-sea-smell recall a happiness forever lost. But paradisal memory can be overpowering (a persistent theme in M.'s work), inducing in the rememberer a torpor, a paralysis even, that estranges him from life and from others. As the poet would write some forty years later in "Voice That Came with the Coots," "Memory's / no sin, so long as it serves some purpose. After that, / it's the laziness of moles, degradation / mouldering on itself."

Here, with the growing awareness that return to the past is impossible, the paradisal fantasy shatters, and the gusting wind brings with it, not death but life, a fresh commitment to the precious reality of the fleeting present. The deadening weight of an irrecoverable past yields to the recognition of the beauty and color (vividly perceived now against the sky's indifferent pallor) of a never-to-be-repeated morning. And the loneliness of a man entrapped in the past is annulled as the wind reveals the *miracle*—communities *(gruppo di abitati)* of men able, although (or because) physically and spiritually famished *(affamati)*, to celebrate the brief *festa* of their lives. Just as the beloved's hair at first spreads its filigree against a pale sky—foreground against background—so now the vivid holiday colors of "bunting and banners" festoon the *paese* as it suddenly appears *(ed or fa vivo)* from the mountain haze presumably dispersed by the (dawn?) breeze fluttering the banners and ruffling the bunting.

Shoot stretching from the wall . . . (1926?)

Reprise and deepening of themes first advanced in "The Lemon Trees" and "Almost a Fantasia," and developed in subsequent poems. The shoot sprouting from the wall, like the agave in "Agave on the Cliff" and the "I" of "Chrysalis," is the poet's totemic *semblable* or persona; its/his distress and tension are suggested by *teso* in the first line. The shoot is painfully tautened, stretched between polarities. Above is the vault of heaven to which it points and whose movements, like the pointer of a sundial, it records; below is the earthen plaster *(tonaco)* into which it stubbornly digs its roots. Thus its condition is not unlike that of the poet in "Falsetto": although born of "the race / of those who cling to the shore," his aspiration outward and upward toward sea and sky is expressed in his admiration for Esterina. But the suffering of the sprig is exacerbated by the boredom it endures, trapped in that monotonous circularity of clocked or measured time that everywhere in M. expresses spiritual "blockade," the intolerable tedium *(noia)* of a Limbo life-in-death, as in "the pageant of hours / too much alike" in "Almost a Fantasia" or the ever-thickening "winter's tedium" of "The Lemon Trees").

Breakthrough *(varco)* into miracle comes in the experience elliptically indicated by the white space between stanzas. Night— the twilight of the fifth line—breaks the cycle and (reminiscent of the lifting sea breeze in "Wind and Banners") revives the shoot, releasing it from the dreariness of diurnal time through a simple natural event. In M.'s immanent world Nature is the great source and spring of all miracle; the Clizia of the later poems, for instance, is herself a natural force. Veiled at night with gossamer mesh (spiderweb? dew? hoarfrost?), the sprig shimmers in the dawn light. Revived, it (and the man whom it conceals, who peers *through* it, *in* it, at the world disclosing itself) sees the world afresh, perceives the miracle manifest in ordinary things: a real three-master on its everyday business ("ballasted with crew and catch"), freely moving on its charted course, tranquilly accepting its transient passage ("cuts the water and leaves no trace"). Thus, like "Falsetto," the poem closes by juxtaposing in real but momentary harmony the contrapuntal worlds of sea and land, day and night, heaven and earth, self and others. And by closing as he has, the poet can now modulate into the celebrated sequence of short lyrics that follow, in which the intricately shifting relations of those polarities will be further inflected and explored.

CUTTLEFISH BONES

Don't ask me for words . . . (1923)

E.M., in a letter to Angelo Barile (August 12, 1924):

"You're right. *'Don't ask me for words . . .'* is a kind of key to my 'rondels,' and in fact will close them, conclusion and commentary. . . ." [In M.'s original plan, the shorter *Ossi* were to contain, in addition to this poem, five lyrics: *"Bring me the sunflower . . .," "Maybe one morning . . .," "To laze at noon . . .," "Don't take shelter in the shade . . .,"* and *"I think again of your smile . . ."*]

As M.'s acknowledged "key" to the earlier group of shorter *Ossi* and his declaration of a new poetics that rejected Romantic notions of poetry as vatic pronouncement, the poem has inevitably received very extensive critical attention and extremely diverse interpretations. Among English commentators, see Cary (254–55), and also West (72–4), who casts light on M.'s revealing use of the subjunctive in shaping a poetics of ironic self-doubt and negative velleity. But the two most comprehensive treatments of the poem are those of Almansi and Merry, and Huffman, from whose studies the following commentaries have been excerpted:

Almansi and Merry (27–30):

> [Montale's] true manifesto [is not "The Lemon Trees," but] *"Don't ask me for words . . .,"* first of twenty-two short *"Ossi."* The poetics of near-silence in this *osso* will exert a corresponding formative influence over the way Montale's major themes are treated. . . . The peremptory tone of the opening imperative may well distract the reader from the far more striking and alarming declaration that follows it, slyly tucked away in apposition with those garish statements described as "bright as fire" and "radiant as a crocus." This declaration comes with the modest adjective *"informe"* (formless, shapeless), lurking behind its noun at the very end of the first phrase as if to conceal its vital declaration of insignificance. The poet is not only stating that a loud and declamatory poetics trivializes the world of nature with facile definitions. What Montale is saying is more far-reaching: there is nothing we can state or deny; nothing to confirm or reject. A single piece of marble, or a single composition is no longer capable of defining some laborious concept, as Michelangelo suggested, because the concept itself has abandoned the field, leaving an ill-formed space in its stead. If our soul is "formless," then any formal declaration is a betrayal, since it fixes a form or seals a meaning to which the soul has no intrinsic right. The poet is no longer faced by the trans-human which cannot be expressed *per verba,* "through words," as Dante says (*Par-*

adiso I, 70); it is the human part of us, the nerve-centre of our humanity, which is unmasked as a formless and incomprehensible entity.

This means that the poet is engaged in a double game. On the one hand he seems to be rejecting the reader's desire for some definitive answer to life from art, while at the same time insinuating that no such answer can be given because nothing can reconcile the opposition between what is formless (emotion, thought, and so on) and what is inherently formal (language, art, poetry, metre, rhythm). Thus poetry is bound to fail in the task of reproducing the soul's inner workings; it can only mime its haphazard and variable phenomena. The lesson is that only in chance circumstances can emotion and experience intersect. But the problem becomes even more complex: quite possibly the poet was playing a treble game in [his opening stanza]. This unrealizable statement, written in letters of fire, which Montale pretended to banish from the domain of poetry, is redeemed in the evocative intensity of the simile, because the vulgar inscription in fiery letters is restored in the pathos of a resplendent crocus in a meadow. Even if the first part of the hypothesis *("a lettere di fuoco / lo dichiari")* ["in letters of fire / publish it"] condemned a facile psychologizing poetry, the second, phrased as a simile, re-enacts the old enterprise of casting man and his isolation as a subject fit for poetry, by concentrating on that pathetically single crocus, which stands, like ourselves, in the midst of a grey universe. So the adjective *"informe,"* subordinated by its neutral position in both line and strophe, is redeemed by its conceptual importance. Now the link with the following strophe becomes clearer. The formlessness of our feelings hints enigmatically at some other deeper but equally mysterious *ego* which is totally ignored by the arrogant and self-assured walker. . . .

As usual, the moment of truth occurs at the noon-tide hour (elsewhere *["Don't take shelter . . ."]* Montale will say: *"È ora . . . / di guardare le forme / della vita che si sgretola"* ["Time now to . . . / gaze at the forms of a life / that powders away"]). The shadow cast by this hour is a formless deleted mark, which speaks only to a zone of anguished ignorance in us. The self-assurance of the walker and the attitude of the speaker each exhibit a different mode of self-*un*awareness. The first of these is the mode of arrogant indifference, an over-confident de-coding of the meaning of one's thoughts and motives at the surface-level. The second drastically reduces our self-knowledge to a faint outline of the unknown inner soul. . . . The poet seems to be carrying on two operations in the close of the poem: first of all he is rejecting the vulgar blandishment of a declamatory or resounding eloquent poetics, the kind that romantically assumes for the poet the role of grand interpreter of the world. He declares that he prefers what would now be called "impoverished writing" *(scrittura povera)*. Secondly, the poet is even denying that valid expression can emerge from that humbler way, the way of his stammerings and simple word-choices. Hence poetry is caught in a dilemma: eloquence and grandeur are rejected; but simplicity is also wrong. What is left is a negative poetics, a task of speaking which becomes the task of staying silent. Hence the last two lines, and hence the closing mockery of all poetry by this one poet who declares in lines of great paradox that verse can only dig its own grave, strain towards its own autonomous *cupio dissolvi*.

Claire de C. L. Huffman (76–9):

Interestingly, this is a poem formed by the negation in its opening and closing lines. An interpretation based on paraphrase would see the final lines as a simple modification of the first ones: the poet cannot only not give a word to define man, but can also only say what man is not, and what he does not want. Yet the poem does give a form to man, who is "formless," "amorphous" in character, and "indefinable," and even defines that form, no matter how negatively conceived: "the most intense heat of summer," "noonday burning," imprints man's shadow on the crumbling, decaying wall. These words, evocative almost *despite* their polemical framework, rise and emerge as though by resistance to an idea. They effectively deny the initial *topos* of inexpressibility: they alone provide the context in which the imperative can be released as a dramatic utterance. The concluding statement, the opening negative imperative, and the image are in no way clearly separable.

The poem opens by appearing to be based on an interest in the possibilities of particular words, or in language generally—*"la parola"* (word, speech, doctrine, even poetic language). Thus, the syllable that must be dry as a branch would seem to illustrate the poet's announced theme, and represent a poetry that will resist easy musicality, even all music, will be dry in personal expression, in tone and sound, and bare as the bareness of some existential condition. But the image of the shadow imprinted on the "decaying" wall, while yet carrying an assertive quality—the wall is "exposed in bare patches," is no longer "plastered" with untruth— masks a perceptible kind of nostalgic regret for the transitory nature of human life. In the guise of asking how one is to write, Montale deals with the question of why one writes, to which there can be no rational answer. There is no resolution to the condition of a world in which the true printer is burning heat and the blank page is a crumbling wall; or to the fact that the wall, crumbling in time, suggests irreversible deterioration. The answers can only be poetic: the Romantic search for immortality or the modern expression of individual anxiety. Thus, the *tone* of the first and last lines, rather than their content, is the poetic correlative of the poet's dilemma and in a sense suggests an answer to it. Paraphrase is inadequate when faced with the poem's procedure. It commands one not to expect language to state man's predicament, and says that the poet cannot use certain kinds of words, but, rather, it concludes, only "dry" ones, in a minimal, reductive poetry, "dry as a branch"; but, ironically, it gives, even simultaneously in the opening lines, exclamatory and meditative phrases that transcend elements of polemic, and images that rise from the polemic. . . .

To laze at noon . . . (1916)

Almansi and Merry (30–4):

The one poem by Montale which most Italian devotees of poetry know by heart is *"Meriggiare pallido e assorto" ["To laze at noon . . ."]*, the earliest . . . poem in the collection. . . .
   It was a traditional habit of critics to identify the quintessence of his poetry in this poem and in this particular landscape: rocky, barren, arid, extrapolated either from his own native Liguria or from a Liguria of his imaginative memory, the mythical land of childhood that is part of the baggage which we all carry around with us. And this landscape was to be seen in the unemotional certainty of a noon-

day's light. This was the landscape as a prey, something to seize and to latch on to, as Montale himself declared in his own "Imaginary Interview": "But in 1916 I had already composed my first fragment *tout entière à sa proie attaché:* '*Meriggiare pallido e assorto. . . .*' That prey was, quite obviously, my personal landscape." The French expression refers to a celebrated line uttered by Phèdre in Racine's play, but Montale makes an implausible leap from the inward attachment of the Racinian character to a grip on the outside landscape by the twentieth-century poet. In this critical dimension it was quite an obvious choice to select as a fundamental statement of Montale the first line of the poem, and the very first word in the line as its key—"*meriggiare.*" . . .

There are many *meriggiari* in Montale, either stated with one of the banner-words such as "*mezzogiorno*" [noon] or "*canicola*" [midday sun, dog days], or implicitly hinted at in the text. This very frequency and the facile temptation of a straight interpretation . . . has blandished many critics, holding out to them a seductive solution of all the critical problems of *Ossi di seppia* which would thus be summarized in the glory of "noondayness" and the anguish of aridity. Yet . . . the interpretative key never fits twice running into the Montalean door: we arrive at a positive and negative quality, at opposite poles; at a sun which helps vision and a sun which also blinds, a sun for salvation and a sun for damnation, in short—a yellow and a black sun. Ultimately Montale works in the tension between these two alternatives, offered almost between the lines of the text to the reader. . . .

Begin by considering the opening lines and the inseparability of the two adjectives, *pallido-e-assorto*. These deliberately imprecise epithets suggest a meaning which the two words taken on their own do not legitimately possess. The combination is not used to suggest the sum of their respective meanings, but to convey a meaning which lies elsewhere, in the margins of the text. For *meriggiare* is neither specifically "*pallido,*" nor "*assorto,*" but instead the whole expression *meriggiare pallido-e-assorto* hints at an unusual, unnatural calm of the physical surroundings, a vista of objects immersed in themselves, soaked in the thought of themselves: "*L'acqua come noi pensa se stessa*" ["the water, like ourselves, reflects on itself"], Montale will say in a poem from *Satura* ["The Arno at Rovezzano"]. Man is definitely cut out from this nature and can only accost it tentatively, practically on tip-toe, in his hope that it will yield something of its secret life to him.

The word *meriggiare,* itself in a precarious balance between the status of verb and noun, set in a sentence apparently lacking a grammatical subject, and thus with an ironic challenge against all normal syntactic and poetic expectations, opens a series of infinitive tenses. But these tenses refer to human activities from which Man himself has been banished. They impose the act of seeing without a see-er, the act of listening without a pair of ears, of spying without an inquisitive mind to do the spying.

This perceivable, noticeable world challenges not only grammatical rules, but any sort of faith in the poetic validity of mimesis (straight artistic representation of man's physical surroundings). Natural objects are organized in a series of phonetic clashes dominated by the close inter-action of plosive and guttural consonants: *pruni / sterpi / schiocchi / serpi,* (and only the onamatopoeic *frusci* breaks the aggressive articulation of the rhyme and sounds here). Even in these lines the words are marvellously imprecise, *mots injustes . . .* harmonized into the discourse by semantic effects which do not depend on the single word but on the meaning-quotient of rhymes, cadence, assonance and rhythm. . . . Consider for instance the expression *"schiocchi di merli"* [scolding of blackbirds], imposed on the reader not so much by a zoological fact as by the formal inevitability of that particular pairing of guttural explosions. Everything is ecologically improbable but poetically viable and therefore inevitable in this composition, which recreates the impossible cohabitation of Noah's Ark: birds and ants, a sea decked with fish scales, and those wildly implausible cicadas. For now the words are assuming control over the text: *"assorto"* demands—and gets—an answering *"orto."* The same relationship holds between the words *"sterpi"* and *"serpi."* The sound uttered by the cicadas is not determined by their vocal organs but by the tempting fascination of the alliterative series in *-i-* (*"tremuli schricci / di cicale dai calvi picchi"*); their habitat too is merely imposed by the logic of the rhymes.

We can accept the provenance in Dante for Montale's *"spiar le file di rosse formiche"* [spying the files of red ants], and our understanding of Montale's personal *bestiario* is enriched by comparing the two passages. . . . The Montalean ants, which share the verb *"spiare"* with the Dante passage, also puzzle poet and reader who have to deal with them. Their contradictory behaviour—*"che ora si rompono ed ora s'intrecciano"* [now break up and now entwine]—is incomprehensible; they live in the separate world of nature where the human observer is an ignorant intruder. . . .

If we move from the microcosm of the ants to the macrocosm of the sea, the position is not substantially changed: the sea is not only far removed, but enclosed in an artificial frame, *"tra frondi"* [through leaves], observed as though it made the centre part of a stage-set. Moreover, the image of the sea is oddly followed by the celebrated lines on the cicadas, which in any case are not linkable to the sea (because they live on hill tops), nor to the verb *"osservare,"* as they are invisible though audible. Besides, these abnormal cicadas, quite unlike any other cicadas of countryside or fairy-tale, utter tremulous *schricci* which originate from *"calvi picchi"* (bare mountain-tops). . . .

We come now to the climax of the poem, where all the *data* originating from the external world ought to lead us, the readers, to some metaphysical conclusion. But this conclusion has already been decided for us and for the poet by the logic of rhyme, by the distracting sequence of rhymed words and assonances. In fact, the assonance "-aglia," "-iglia," "-aglio," "-aglia," "-iglia," in the closing strophe, takes command of the situation and reduces the poet's freedom of action by imposing that particular discovery which suits the phonetic pattern of the strophe itself. The long and painfully drawn-out hendiadys, *"com'è tutta* la vita e il suo travaglio / *in questo seguitare una muraglia"* eventually finds a solution in the aggressive jags of glass which thus become the definitive image of our human condition and allow the line to become established at the centre of the Montalean symbolic glossary. Reviewing the lesson of the poem, we can say that author and reader alike are left with no choice: they are obliged by the text to believe in the symbolic force of the *muraglia* (barrier-wall, rampart). . . .

★   ★   ★

W.A.: *at the tips of the tiny sheaves.* My rendering may raise eyebrows. Commentators and translators alike have preferred to take *biche* as "heaps" rather than "sheaves," though either is possible. The "heaps" (or "piles") would be anthills; the "sheaves" would refer to the sheaflike look of vetch-leaves. That the *biche* here are "sheaves," not "heaps," is more than suggested, I think, by an allusion to Dante (*Inf.* xxix, 64–6), evident in the use of the identical rhyme-words: *formiche / biche.* "I do not think it was a greater sorrow," says Dante, "to see the people in Aegina all sick [devastated by the plague] . . . and afterwards restored from the seed of ants / than it was to see, through that dark valley [in Hell], the spirits lying in diverse sheaves":

> . . . *si ristorar di seme di* formiche:
> *ch'era a veder per quella oscura valle*
> *languir gli spirti per diverse* biche.

Singleton comments ad loc.: *"biche:* 'Shocks,' sheaves of grain piled one upon another, once a familiar scene at harvest time. . . ." Finally, the sense of impasse so strong in the poem is confirmed if we visualize the ants as piling up helplessly at the tips of the leaves rather than at their anthills (which are after all organized so as to obviate gridlock).

Don't take shelter in the shade . . . (1922)

Second in the collection of early *Ossi brevi* entitled *Rottami* ("Fragments," or perhaps "Flotsam"), this beautifully crafted lyric of aspiration toward *varco* ["breakthrough" or "passage"] varies and widens the intricating themes of the suite. Thus it looks forward to *"Bring me the sunflower . . .,"* *"Splendor of noon outspread . . .,"* and above all to "Moiré," but also converses with contrasting variations in *"I think again of your smile . . ."* and *"Once again the canebrake . . ."* In the latter poems the subject is lost paradisal love remembered; here it is an exhortation to love addressed to a *tu* who is likened to the small hawk familiarly known as the windhover. It is also the poet's glancing but unmistakable challenge to himself, via the mediating figure of the Muse-as-beloved, to abandon the comfort of his familiar parish of reality and reach out toward the (Dantesque) ardors of the heights.

Reference points are provided by familiar polarities: noonday sun versus leafy shelter, daring versus timidity and/or inertia, the world above *(lassù)* versus the world below *(quaggiù)*. The poem begins with a typically Montalean negative, but it is one that contains a strong, not merely wistful, positive imperative. Thus in the first stanza the poem's "tu" is adjured *not* to abandon her natural domain—the dense *(fólto)* enclosure of the canebrake (passive isolation in the security of old certainties and "realities"). By the last stanza, however, this injunction becomes not merely a passionate yearning for *varco* but a momentary illusion of *varco* almost achieved. For one astonishing instant, the soaring imagination catches a glimpse of the miracle—that transcendence that, for M., occurs only when *shared* life is lived at peak intensity.

The intervening stanzas chart the narrator's escape from blockade, for it is he—propelled by the aspiration implicit in his imperatives—not the "tu," who does the ascending. Understanding of his ascent depends upon our recognizing the Idealist (Dantesque) thought on which it rests. "Gaze" *(guardare),* he urges, "at the forms of a life / that powders away" *(si sgretola).* The subject of "powders" is not *(pace,* Valentini) "forms," but "life." Life is temporal process and change, whereas forms—the idealist forms of Plato, Aristotle, or Dante-via-Aquinas—are timelessly enduring universals. And in M.'s poetry the process of life is everywhere represented as one of transience, temporal attrition, or erosion. The result of this process is residue: ashes, flotsam, crumblings, flakes, husks, detritus, powder, dust. But this residue, these "dead ends" can, in dissolution and recombination, be revived. Death, as Bakhtin observed, is pregnant with life. True form, *inward* form, is the universal that animates particular phenomena—the *anima* or "life" that survives, persisting in the residues of outward forms. Many years later, in "Little Testament" *(The Storm and Other Things),* M. would write: "A story only survives in ashes, / persistence is only extinction . . . that faint glow catching fire / was not the striking of a match." In the blinding light of noon it is *outward* forms that dissolve (see *"Splendor of noon outspread . . .,"* where "too much light" causes objects to melt into a "tawny shimmer"). What surrounds "us" is more sensed than seen: an iridescent cloud of dust *(pulviscolo),* light-irradiated particles (i.e., in*form*ed matter) through which, all but blinded, "we pass" on our way to *varco*.

But transcendence is negative as well as positive. *Varco* is a "passage" that leads down as well as up. Upward toward that spiritual light "where blond transparencies rise / and life evaporates as essence." Downward into black nothingness, to the *nulla* of the abyss or Baudelaire's *gouffre* perhaps, but above all to that nether Nirvana of sensual immersion and "oceanic feeling" celebrated by D'Annunzio.

In the fourth stanza decision is made for *varco* upward to the light-world of the Forms—a decision once again suggested by a negative ("let's *not* throw our strayed lives / to a bottomless abyss"), itself presumably triggered not only by the prospect of the abyss, but by a sense of futility and that *lonely* errancy that is conveyed by the Italian word *randage* (but not by English "stray"). Ultimately of course either form of transcendence is destructive, since, for M., we become, and remain, human only by enduring the conflicting claims made upon the psyche by the two warring transcendental extremes. If the "death" implicit in downward transcendence is obvious enough, it is equally present in its upward form. "The transcendental 'I,' " M. later observed, "is light that illuminates only a very small space in front of us, a light that carries us toward a nonindividual, and therefore nonhuman, condition."

I think again of your smile . . . (1923)

The poem was originally dedicated to Baris Kniaseff, and was third in the sequence of "Rottami." The most searching English account of the poem is that of Claire de C. L. Huffman (110–12). The poem, she writes,

> announces in its title that its subject is memory; the poet seems to celebrate the memory and the exceptional nature of a friend. . . . But if we look at this poem closely . . . Montale's interest is not directly in the purported subject of the poem, the memory of a particular smile. It becomes less important to the poem than other concerns, other images, and an uneasy state of mind.
>
> The lines *"un' acqua limpida / scorta per avventura tra le petraie d'un greto"* ["a pool of water / glimpsed by chance in the torrent's gravel bed"] seem to be complimentary metaphor in which attention falls on the quality of the friend's smile. In fact, the metaphor is so articulated, one might say overarticulated, that the reader's attention correctly falls elsewhere. First, the phrase *"scorta per avventura"* throws

203

stress on the chance discovery of a positive element, a trickle of "limpid water" among the stones in the gravelly, dry "riverbed" or "bank." Were we to make the error of taking this metaphor as one chiefly concerned with a smile, we would be confronted with grotesque associations among a loved and smiling face and a dried-up "rockbed" and its aridity; the additional elements ("tiny mirror," etc.) would seem overextended. In fact, the subject, the smile, gets lost in, or at best only typifies, the discovery of something positive in negative and reluctant vehicles, "heaped stones" in a dried-out "riverbed," which themselves may stand for anything—the passage of time, the poet's memory, other memories, life itself. Montale is thus largely unconcerned with the possibilities and functions of figurative language and imagination, in unities or fusions of thought and perception; rather, he is interested in the way life only very rarely offers itself to him by yielding a single, seemingly unrepeatable good that does not originate within himself. . . .

The smile and the friend diminish in significance in relation to the poet's predisposition, which is filled with the idea that some people are graced—even in adversity— and others not, and that the poet is excluded from some particular and unnamed grace that guides others through life. All of life, apart from the disembodied memory, the smile that lives in some present time . . . and alone is capable of engendering the "quiet white sky," is negative. All is *"i crucci estrosi,"* "capricious sufferings," and escape lies in submerging anxieties and finding an *"ondata di calma,"* a rare "calm" for Montale. The animation does not depend upon the poet, however, and, as we have seen, not even on sensation or imagination. The lines "the candor of your image probes my graying memory / like the spear of a young palm" show that a memory lives only by insinuating itself into the "memory" of the poet, carving itself in the "gray"— "gloomy," "passive," and "sad"—mind in opposition to all other reality, so that, once again, difficulty is transferred to the mind and its ambiguous, rather passive, space. . . . The poet seeks to escape isolation by holding onto an exceptional image that must itself be active and subtly aggressive, to overcome his passivity. This active element is almost kinesthetic, reinforced by the consonants of *"schietto"* [sincere, candid] and by the visual sound con-

veyed by the repeated vowel "i" in the last lines. As in the
later "Motets," Montale is making memory visual—*"cima"*
. . . *"giovinetta"* [spear . . . young palm]—against the
grayness of his own mind.

What I ask, my life . . . (1924?)

Two contrasting stanzas divided by an eloquent white space
that the poet straddles as he explores his own contradictions.
Straddling expresses moral and metaphysical tension, a tension that
must be lived out. The quarrel between immanence and transcen-
dence in the psyche was one that M. felt could not be optimisti-
cally brushed aside. "We need," he wrote, "to live our contradictions
without evasions, but also without too much enjoyment . . ."—
that is, without heroic posturing, that flaunting of tragic suffering
that M. detested. But refusal to abide the tension of one's contra-
dictions meant rejecting fully human existence; it could be obviated
only by ceasing to straddle.

The contradictions posed by the poem are, on one hand, a life
of incessant activity, the round of mere busyness whose result is
material comfort and certainty, plausible and predictable; on the
other, quietism, an untroubled calm enabled by renouncing the
turmoil of passion, above all love, and, by so doing, ceasing to
live at the mercy of recurrent emotional storms. Step by step, the
poem probes the alternatives. If the poem finally comes down on
the side of passion, the poet's yearning for tranquillity makes it
clear that, even while leaning toward passion, he is still "strad-
dling." If the first two lines flatly reject the life of busy ambition,
the next two lines specify its flaws—restless circularity *(giro inquieto),*
a tedium of repetition that levels high and low, bitter and sweet,
"wormwood / and honey" in deadening apathy.

The very restlessness, however, reveals that generalized dis-
satisfaction that implies unsatisfied craving for Plato's "something
else" *(ti allo).* No doubt the seemingly resigned atony (see Cary,
256) could be construed as Svevo-like vocational *senilità*—"the state
of being of whoever feels he has already lived for himself and oth-
ers, suffered and lived for all." But the clear link here *(non chiedo)*
with the positively charged negatives of *"Don't ask me for words
. . ."* *(Non chiederci)* suggests neither humble acceptance nor "Pro-
methean" resignation. The life first described is not the life one

wants but rather what one "settles for." Tedium may be a constant of M.'s world, but so is the persistent (because dialectically related) yearning for *varco* and transcendence (see note on *"There Triton surges . . ."*)—or the feel of the life-blood quickening at one's pulses.

Quietism, as the second stanza hints, is not the answer. But those who have suffered the vicissitudes of passion, requited or not, know the appeal of liberation from its tyranny. Numbness and passivity have their charms, as the first two lines indicate; but even while acknowledging this, the poet delicately distances himself by shifting from the "I" of the first stanza to (the impersonal) "heart" of the second. If this "heart" presumes to look down upon *(tiene a vile)* all motion, the poet also seems to be chiding such presumption. That is, the busyness faulted in the first stanza is now widened to include *motions* of the heart—e-*motion.* Confirmation of this subtle modulation toward passion lies in the untranslatable phrase, *squassato da transalimento.* Unpacked, this means something like "violently shaken by light tremors provoked by unexpected feeling." It is the shock of unexpected emotion which the last two lines express, as the verbal torpor created by the drowsy slowness of the third line—*Così suona talvolta nel silenzio*—is explosively shattered in the fourth. (For a strikingly parallel, see "Stanzas" in *The Occasions:* "as when the silence of a drowsing / piazza is sometimes shattered / by an explosion of doves.") Now we know where the poet, at least for the moment, is to be found. Not stiffly straddling his contradictions, but flexibly adapting, moving to and fro, back and forth (or up and down), according to changing needs and feelings.

Bring me the sunflower . . . (1923)

Almansi and Merry (34–5):

> [This poem is] the most striking statement in Montale's contradictory solar mythology. The sunflower, which foreshadows the strange figure of Clizia, enamoured of Apollo, *"che a guardar lo sol si gira"* (who turns to contemplate the sun), points both to salvation although the mystic path might lead to the great pool of not-being, to the *ex-stasis* of self-annulment *("svanire è dunque,"* etc.), and also to the damnation of madness *("il girasole impazzito di luce").* The sun, the light, the heat are operative on both fronts.

. . . In previous poems (for example, *"Don't ask me for words
. . ."*) . . . culture may lead us to uncertainty, ignorance
and darkness, but the opposite thrust to light and knowl-
edge may be equally disappointing. Moving towards the
light may well involve the self-purification of greater light-
ness, which in its turn leads to the supreme spirituality of
colours and musical sounds; but the ultimate goal is still
nothingness. In Montale's world everything ends up in this
kind of dispersion into a void. Thus the delirium of the sea
"sale agli astri ormai" ["rises at last to the stars," the last line
of the seventh poem in the suite "Mediterranean"]. A
strangled life is carried, in another poem, *"con la cenere degli
astri"* [*"with the* ashes of the stars," the last words of
"Arsenio"]. To disappear, in the lines quoted above, is "the
ultimate adventure." . . . Hence Montale's myth of the
sunflower has nothing to share with an extroverted, good-
natured immersion in a vitalizing sun, but involves . . . a
state of *not*-saying, a point of self-erasure. All this, despite
the fundamental ambiguity of the last line of the second
strophe, where *"ventura"* is deliberately presented in the
simultaneous guise of "good fortune," "misfortune" and
"adventurous chance." The darkness which extinguishes
or the light which illuminates—both lead to parallel results:
either that which we are becomes mad with light or it
becomes enmeshed *"in una sola / ghiacciata moltitudine di morti"*
[in a single / frozen multitude of the dead; see "Arsenio"].
Therefore nothingness and void await reader and poet alike
in the Janus-like image of dark death or radiant sun light.

I have often met . . . (undated)

One of the most anthologized lyrics of the *Ossi brevi,* until
very recently memorized by generations of Italian school children.
The poem itself is a good example, not of M.'s vocational *senilità*
(see note on "What I ask, my life . . ."), but rather of a stubbornly
lived stoical "pragmatism" (in William James's sense: neither
rationalistically "tender-minded" nor scientifically "tough-
minded"). The "evil of living" *(male di vivere)* is suggested only
by images—papering leaf, strangled brook, fallen horse (an allu-
sion perhaps to Raskolnikov's vision of evil?). Existential, not moral,
it hints at transience, the sense of impasse or finitude, the decay of
physical beauty and strength. The good that emerges in the second

stanza is essentially moral, a bleakly disciplined acceptance of life's ills and of the cosmic or divine Indifference to human achievement and aspiration as evoked by the statue (the dormant, not dead, memorial of human greatness), the cloud, the soaring hawk. If such acceptance implies skepticism and even resignation, it also suggests tenuous, skeptical hope and a persistence equal to that hope, as in the final stanza of *"To laze at noon . . ."*

What you knew of me . . . (undated)

Ironically assertive or assertively ironic self-exploration, strikingly similar in image and tone to Eliot's persistent depiction of himself as a disappearing *persona,* a phantom or "hollow man." Compare, for instance, the negative / positive conclusion of "The Hollow Men" or *"Mélange Adultère de Tout."* From one shadow-self to another, the persona proceeds at last to a birth-death, negative only if the reader ignores the positives latent in "Not with a bang but a whimper" and *"cénotaphe."* In much the same way M. suggests the positive achievement that, typically and ironically, underlies the apparently negative *dépouillement* of his persona. Thus the poem's "I" feels an entrapment or solipsism "so intense that he speaks of himself in the past definite or historical sense" (Cary, 256). But there is surely more to him than the self-parodying grimace of a precocious *raté.* As critics have observed, ignorance for M. is a positive trait, almost synonymous with a natural, unself-conscious (and essentially Socratic) innocence. (For the idea see note on the next poem, *"There Triton surges . . ."*) Ignorance is precious to the "I" because it preserves the "unquenched fire"— i.e., the innate, enduring energies of life. The last stanza, however, intimates the impossibility, at least for the Montalean "I," of self-transcendence by breaking through to that ultimate ignorance. Nonetheless the transcendental aspiration is *there* as the self-sacrifice implied in the last line ("I'd give it [my shade] to you, gladly") clearly suggests, even though as so often it is undercut by the all-too-knowledgeable doubt conveyed by that wistful subjunctive *potessi.*

There Triton surges . . . (undated)

The Triton is a torrent in the vicinity of Portovenere, a former fishing village, now a fashionable resort commanding a superb view of the island of Palmaria and the cliffs of M.'s Cinque Terre. According to legend it was at Portovenere (the ancient *Portus Veneris*) that St. Peter disembarked on first reaching Italy. The temple of Venus that once stood there reportedly sank when the apostle celebrated Mass. To this site "at the sources," where pagan and Christian mingle and the ancient sea god Triton survives in the torrent that bears his name, the adult city-man returns to visit and perhaps renew himself. There habitual certainties (the "firm / outlines, plausible looks, possessions" of *"What I ask, my life . . ."*) fall away, to be succeeded by doubt, uncertainty, indecision. Elsewhere in M.'s poetry these traits are often presented as corrosive or paralyzing; here instead they are positive and restorative. Thus it is a childlike uncertainty *(dubbiezza)* and absence of self-regard that guide the visitor back to innocence, ignorance, silence, the sources from which, for M., all honest speech (i.e., poetry), all true individuality spring. (For variants on the idea see particularly *"What you knew of me . . . ,"* *"The children's farandole . . . ,"* *"Your hand was trying . . . ,"* the sea-teachings of "Mediterranean" and notes thereon.) Here at the sources "every future hour is old"; only by reimmersing oneself in innocence and ignorance can one hope to become a true individual. For M. the possession of a human face always means that identity has been won and true individual features have replaced the mask (see note on "Sarcophagi" and "To my Mother" in *The Storm and Other Things*). The social "one" becomes a person, an undeniable *this*. But the child is father to the man; individuality requires one to leave the child's paradisal world and return to the here-and-now, the adult life of decision, will, speech, and reason. Whether the "you" of this poem will later resume his masked life depends on what is made of that ambiguous "assume" *(assumere)* in the last line. A face, like responsibilities, may be honorably "assumed"; it may also be assumed, i.e., "put on," like a mask. The ironies of Eliot's Prufrock ("time / to prepare a face to meet the faces that you meet") are likely to dispose most Anglo-American readers to take "assume" in the second, deprecatory sense; the Italian word, however, leaves matters open. The ambiguity is characteristically Montalean.

I know that moment . . . (undated)

Lyric of negative *varco*. Instead of breaking through to "the miraculous moment," the poem centers on the hurt and anguish concealed beneath the stolidity and "plausible features" of the individual's social face or mask. In either case, the result is impasse: the radical inability of poetry to express the inexpressible. Shared grief (as in *"Your hand was trying . . ."*) may create a reciprocal understanding; solitary pain, as in this poem, immures and isolates. For variations on M.'s poetics (or antipoetics) of silence, see notes to *"There Triton surges . . .," "Your hand was trying . . .," "Happiness won . . .," "Maybe one morning . . .,"* and elsewhere.

Splendor of noon outspread . . . (1924?)

E.M., in a letter to Angelo Barile (August 12, 1924):

> . . . besides the twenty *Ossi [brevi],* the book will also contain fifteen lyrics, not at all brief—anything but!—and extremely varied; some of them, from the period of "Seacoasts," are more "singable" and pleasing; the image of me that will emerge from the book will seem less coherent to you but larger and more complex; and yours truly *[il sottoscritto]* will be revealed as more of a "troubador" than a sophist and workshop-poet. . . . In September *Opere e i giorni* will publish . . . an *osso*—my best yet, indeed the only one that really pleases me: "Splendor of noon outspread . . ."

Once again (as in *"To laze at noon . . ."*) the blinding glory of a Mediterranean high noon *(l' ora del meriggio)* with its stunned silence and burning desolation provides still another of those liminal occasions when consciousness dissolves and everyday objects are shorn of solidity, even shadow, blurring into a formless "tawny shimmer." Universal torpor afflicts land and sea; the poet too, at this "high noon" of his life ("My day, then, is not done . . ."), appears to relish the prospect of fading into "the loveliest hour," the white blank that lies "beyond the closure." Both tone and sense—the anticipation of Nirvana-like negative transcendence in a "whitewashed sunset"—seem designed to recall the reflections prompted by the sunflower a few poems earlier:

> Dark things are drawn to brighter,
> bodies languish in a flowing
> of colors, colors in music. To vanish,
> then, is the venture of ventures.

The arid noon of the first stanza is beautiful, a glorious sterility whose effect is the sapped wistfulness of the death-wish in the second stanza. This bleakness of tone then spills over into the third: "Drought all around." A colon follows, as though the desolation were about to be gathered into in a comprehensive general image or statement. But instead, the poem veers to a "sign" of faint but still audible affirmation. This unpredictable semantic "swerve," profoundly Montalean, is generated not by a penchant for rhetorical surprises but by the revulsion of repudiated life itself against such desolation. The noonday drought of the first two stanzas is so intolerable that a "relic / of life" stirs in the poet, signaling its presence in a "sign": the blue flash of a kingfisher hovering over some other "relic" still alive in the waste below—a glance at the reliquary-crucible of *"In limine."* Whether the "sign" causes, or is caused by, the affirmation, is irrelevant. In M.'s poetics of immanence, signs rarely function metaphorically, but rather metonymically, stating or suggesting the identity of object and subject, "you" and "I," and later, poem and triggering "occasion." In short, the last two lines transform the kingfisher into a sign of hope. However tenuous or illusory, that hope is a necessity. Men who inhabit a wasteland, whether Eliot's ("If only there were water amongst the rock . . .") or M.'s, live only in the prospect of rain, physical and / or spiritual; but what to M. matters more than rain is the relished expectation of it. "My genre," M. wrote *a propos* of his "turnkey" poem, *"In limine,"* "is entirely *a waiting for the miracle"* [M.'s emphasis].

Happiness won . . . (undated)

Poetry and poems about writing poetry are in M. almost always statements about living. Writing poetry is painfully frustrating because, despite the poet's best efforts, he is denied "absolute expression"; the veil of language cuts him off from "definitive *quid"* (see note on *"Maybe one morning . . ."*), from what Pavese once called "the word that translates everything." Now and then the miracle occurs; the veil parts for one brief instant as poem and poet seem to "break through," but then closes, leaving the poet with the disillusion inherent in even the finest work. All effort is somehow undone (see "The moment that spoils months of labor is here," in *"Haul your paper boats . . ."*), or the provoking vision is withdrawn (as in the last lines of *"The windlass creaks . . ."*). The inexpressible is to poetry what happiness is to life: no matter how close one comes to it, it slips away: fragile, precarious, elusive. The breakthrough thus ends in the banality of ordinary existence, the ordinariness made drearier by the intoxicating dream of *varco*, while the poet's hope of sustaining a poem at peak intensity dissolves into prosiness, into "literature":

> But moldy dictionary words
> are all I have, and that voice of mystery
> dictated by love grows faint,
> turns literary, elegiac.
>
> [*"If I could only force . . ."* in "Mediterranean"]

Poetry, like happiness, lies wholly in the pursuit, in the risky effort to get closer to what eludes one: to *see, feel, touch,* and *possess* it. Even if possible, possession is brief and ruinous: the memory confers only pain, the tedium of ordinary days tormented by the contrastingly dreamlike memory of what one has lost—a child's ball vanishing between the buildings.

Again the canebrake . . . (undated)

The poem provides a revealing example of the way in which, stanza by stanza, M. develops and modulates his themes. The first stanza creates a sense of incipient *varco* as the canebrake pokes fresh shoots into (an early spring?) sky that offers no impediment (*non si ragna*—literally, "not webbed by wispy streaks of cloud")—and the fruit trees probe their way beyond constricting walls. But with the stanza's final comma-weighted words, *all' afa stagna,* imminent breakthrough is blunted by the muggy staleness *(stagna)* of gathering haze. This oppressive heat spills over into the second strophe, bringing a sense of failed *varco* and blockade in the final line. Then, briefly, the sultriness arouses hope of rain. But the "expectation" (for M.'s poetics of "waiting for the miracle," see note to *"Splendor of noon outspread . . ."*) is abruptly voided by that emphatic *vacua* that closes the first line and anticipates the despair of the fourth. Still, such is the nature of expectation that the hope of rain persists, "encouraged" by the darkening sea and the thunderheads piling up, before collapsing into ashes. The word "ashes" enables the otherwise inexplicable transition to the apostrophe invoking the absent-present beloved (an anticipation of the Clizia figure of *The Occasions* and *The Storm*), which occupies the whole third stanza. Like the drought-born hope of rain, desire for the absent beloved lives on, burning in the ashes of "charred souls." (For M.'s imagery of fire and ashes, see notes to "Sarcophagi," *"Don't take shelter in the shade . . .," "Squander, if you want . . .,"* and "Arsenio.") Just as the sunflower aspires to the sun from which it draws its life, so the lover's longing pursues the beloved into the void that contains her, even though this may mean that the lover himself merges with, becomes the void, a hazy nothingness (see the "wan sunset" of *"Splendor of noon outspread . . ."*) into which his world on "this shore," the world-as-representation, vanishes.

Maybe one morning . . . (1923)

M.'s influence on the mind, imagination, and experience of modern Italy has been, without the slightest exaggeration, immense and radical. Not since Leopardi has any poet so profoundly affected the thought, language, and culture of his contemporaries. The poems, memorized by two generations of school children, continue even now to haunt the Italian mind, providing a point of reference, a model and touchstone by which experience is mediated and organized. In a 1949 essay, *"Tornare nella strada,"* M. would comment on the general failure to acknowledge the persistent subterranean influence of this "second life of art, its obscure pilgrimage through the consciousness and memory of men, its massive flowing back to the life from which art itself drew its first nourishment." One of the most revealing examples of this "second life" is the analysis of *"Maybe one morning . . ."* provided by Italo Calvino on the occasion of M.'s eightieth birthday. Calvino's discussion provides not only a penetrating (and appropriately philosophical) reading of M's poem, but also an extremely suggestive account of the way in which a poem memorized in youth is shaped by, and in turn later shapes, the rememberer. Adapted first by memory, it is subsequently deformed, then vetted and revetted by experience until it becomes indistinguishable from that experience itself—until it becomes, in short, a "life-text." But let Calvino speak for himself:

> As a boy I liked memorizing poems. At school I memorized many—and I now wish I had memorized many more. These poems accompanied me through life in a nearly unconscious mental recital which only years later resurfaced. After completing *liceo,* I spent several years memorizing poems on my own—work by poets who were not then included in the school syllabus. It was in those years that *Ossi di seppia* and *Le occasioni* . . . were beginning to circulate in Italy. So, somewhere around eighteen, I memorized a number of Montale poems: I have forgotten some; others I have carried around with me until the present occasion.
>
> Now, on his birthday, a rereading of Montale naturally sends me back to that archive of poems buried in the memory. . . .
>
> Let me choose one poem which, though lodged in my memory for years and still bearing the marks of that sojourn, best lends itself to immediate, objective reading rather than a quest for those conscious or unconscious autobiographical echoes which Montale's poetry, above all the early poems, arouse in me. For this purpose I have chosen *"Forse un mattino . . ." ("Maybe one morning . . ."),* one of the poems most often spinning on my mental turntable, and one which I recall without the slightest feeling of nostalgia but rather as a poem I am reading for the first time. . . .
>
> *"Maybe one morning . . ."* is a poem that differs from the others, not so much in being a "narrative" poem . . . but because it is devoid of objects and natural emblems, devoid of a specific landscape. A poem, in short, of abstract imagination and insight, something rather uncommon in Montale.
>
> But I notice (to distinguish this poem more sharply from others) that my memory had contributed its own revisions. For me the sixth line began "trees houses streets," not "tree houses hills,"—which now, rereading the poem some thirty-five years later, I see that it says. That is, by substituting "streets" for "hills," I had placed the action in a decidedly urban setting, perhaps because "hills" sounded

too vague, perhaps because the presence of "men who don't look back" suggested a continual parade of people; in short, I saw the world's disappearance as a disappearance of the city rather than of nature. (But now I see that, thanks to memory, the image of crowds rushing down the street, which appears in a pendant composition [*"I know that moment . . ."*] four pages earlier, has bled into this poem.)

Clearly, the source triggering the "miracle" is the natural, i.e., atmospheric, element—the dry, crystalline transparency of the winter air, which renders objects with such clarity that it creates an effect of unreality, as though the halo of mist usually hazing the landscape . . . were identified with the thickness of existence. But this is to anticipate: it is the concreteness of this invisible air, which seems precisely glass, and its self-sufficient solidity, which ends by imposing itself on the world and making it disappear. The glassy air is the poem's true element, and the mental city in which I put it was a city of glass, which becomes so transparent that it disappears. It is the precise specifying of the medium that expresses the sense of nothingness (whereas in Leopardi the lack of such specification achieves the same effect). Or, more exactly, from the initial *"Maybe one morning . . ."* there is a sense of suspension which is not indeterminateness but rather diligent balance, "walking *in* air of dry / glass," as though walking *on* air, in air, in the fragile glass of the air, in the cold morning light, so that in the end we no longer notice that he is suspended in the void.

Through the lilting rhythmical movement, this sense of suspension and concreteness continues into the second line with that colloquial *compirsi,* which the reader is constantly tempted to correct to *compiersi* [the polite form], but then invariably observes that the whole line pivots precisely on that prosy *compirsi,* which softens any emphasis that might verify the "miracle." My ear has always been fond of this line because in my (mental) diction it is sensibly enhanced by having an extra foot, which in fact isn't extra at all, but then my memory often tends to drop syllables. So far as memory is concerned, the most elusive part of the line is *rivolgendomi* (turning back, wheeling), which I sometimes abbreviated to *voltandomi* (turning around) or *girandomi* (wheeling about), and in this way evened out the succession of beats.

A poem imposes itself on our memory (first demanding to be memorized, then remembered), and metrical peculiarities play a decisive role. Montale's use of rhythm has always fascinated me: paroxytone and proparoxytone, slant rhymes, rhymes in unusual positions. . . . Montale is one of those rare poets who know the secret of rhyme as a device for lowering, not heightening, the tone, with unmistakable effects on the meaning. In our poem, the *miracolo* (miracle) which closes the second line is informed by the rhyme with *ubriaco* (drunkard) two lines later, and the entire quatrain is left as it were in uneasy suspension.

The "miracle" is the prime, never-contradicted Montalean theme of the "break in the meshes of the net" (see *"In limine,"* fourth stanza), "the link that doesn't hold" ("The Lemon Trees"); but our poem is one of the few occasions when the *other* truth presented by the poet beyond the continuing wall of the world is revealed in a definable experience. This truth, we might say, is neither more nor less than that of the world's unreality, if this definition doesn't run the risk of generically blurring something reported to us in precise terms. The unreality of the world is the basis of religion, philosophy, and literature, primarily Oriental, but this poem moves in a different epistemological horizon, all clarity and transparency, as in a mental "air of dry / glass."

In his *Phenomenology of Perception,* Merleau-Ponty has some very fine pages on cases in which subjective experience of space is cut off from experience of the objective world (in the dark of night, in dreams, under the influence of drugs, in schizophrenia, etc.). This poem might well provide Merleau-Ponty with an example: space is detached from the world and imposed as it is, empty, limitless. The discovery is hailed by the poet as "miracle," as acquisition of truth as opposed to the "usual illusion." But it is also felt as a terrifying vertigo: "with a drunkard's terror." The man's steps are no longer sustained by an "air of dry / glass": the weighted initial *andando* (walking), is, after his swift wheeling about, resolved into a reeling or tottering—with no further points of reference.

The "suddenly" . . . [in] the second quatrain describes the experience of nothingness in the temporal terms of an instant. Forward motion is now resumed with a real but occasionally elusive landscape; we observe that the poet is merely following one of his many vectors along which other men occupying this space are moving—the "men who don't look back." Hence it is on a complex rectilinear movement that the poem closes.

A doubt remains as to whether these other men also disappeared in that same instant when the world disappeared. Among the objects that "reassemble" are trees but not men (variants in my memory led to different philosophical results). Hence the men might still be there. Just as the world's disappearance does not include the "I" of the poet's "I," so it might also spare every other subject who experiences and judges. The fundamental void is strewn with monads, populated by so many dot-shaped "I's" that, if they turned around, they would discover the illusion; instead they continue to appear as so many backs-in motion, certain of the reality of their trajectory.

In this case we can see the inverse situation of that which is presented, for instance, in "Wind and Banners." There it is human existence which is wholly ephemeral, whereas "the world *is* . . ." in a time never to be repeated. Here, instead, it is only the human presence that persists in the fading away of the world and its causes—presence as hopeless subjectivity since it is either the victim of an illusion or the recipient of the secret of nothingness.

The "void" and the "nothingness" are "at my shoulders," "behind me." This is the essential point of the poem. Not an undefined feeling of dissolution, but rather the building of a cognitive model which is not easily refuted, and which can co-exist in us with other more or less empirical models. The hypothesis can be stated in very simple and rigorous terms: given the dual nature of the space surrounding us—a visible field before our eyes, an invisible field behind us—we define the first as a scrim of illusions; the second as a void which is the world's real substance. We might reasonably expect that the poet, once he has established that there is a void behind him, should extend this discovery in other directions as well. But there is nothing in the text to justify this generalization, whereas the model of dual or bipartite space is never denied by the text; indeed, it is affirmed by the redundance of the third line—"nothingness at my shoulders," "the void / behind me." During my purely mnemonic association with the poem, this redundance at times puzzled me, so I attempted a variant: "the nothingness before me," "the void behind me." That is, the poet turns, sees the road, turns back around, and the void stretches everywhere. But on reflection I understood that a certain poetic pregnancy was lost if the discovery of the road were not localized in that "behind me."

The division of space into two fields—anterior and posterior—is only one of the most elementary human operations on the categories. It is an initial given, common to all animals, and begins very early on the biological ladder, from a time when there were living creatures who developed . . . according to a bipolar scheme, localizing in an extremity those organs that related to the external world: a mouth and nervous termini, some of which will become organs of sight. From then on the world was identified with the anterior field, complemented by an area of unknowability, of *non-world,* of nothingness to the rear of the observer. By shifting position and totting up successive visual fields, the living creature managed to construct for himself a complete, coherent, circular world, but one involving an inductive model for which there will never be satisfying proof.

Man has always suffered from the lack of an eye at the back of his head, and his cognitive position is necessarily problematic since he is never certain of what lies behind him. That is, he cannot ascertain whether the world goes on between the extremes which, by twisting his gaze to right and left, he manages to see. When he is not immobilized, he can turn his head and whole body and find proof that the world is there too, but this also proves that what lies in front of him is always his own visual field, which extends just so many degrees and no further, whereas to his rear there is always a complementary arc in which, at that particular moment, the world might not be. In sum, we pivot on ourselves, pushing our visual field before our eyes, and we never manage to see the nature of the space to which our visual field fails to reach.

The protagonist of Montale's poem succeeds through a combination of factors both objective (air of dry glass) and subjective (receptivity to an epistemological miracle) in turning around so quickly that he manages, let's say, to look at a space still unoccupied by his own visual field. And what he sees is nothingness, the void.

I find the same problematic element, positively (or

negatively, simply by changing the sign) in a legend of the Wisconsin and Minnesota lumberjacks, which Borges cites in his *Fantastic Zoology*. There is an animal called the "Hide-behind," who is always at your back and follows you everywhere when you go out for wood. You turn around but no matter how quickly, the "Hide-behind" is even quicker and has already moved behind you; you will never know what he's like, but he's always there. Borges doesn't cite his source and may himself have invented the story; but this in no way detracts from a hypothetical force which I would call genetic, categorical. We can say that Montale's man is one who has succeeded in turning around and seeing what his "Hide-behind" looks like. And this man is more frightening than any animal; he is nothingness.

It might be objected that this whole discussion ante-dates a basic anthropological revolution of our century— the adoption of rear-view mirrors in cars. Equipped with an eye that looks backwards, motorized man has a guar-antee of the existence of the world behind him. I speak of car mirrors, not of mirrors generally, since in a mirror the world behind us is seen as complementary to ourselves. What the mirror verifies is the presence of the observing subject, to whom the world is an accessory backdrop. It is an objectification of the "I" which the mirror provokes, with the danger of which the myth of Narcissus always reminds us—of drowning into the "I," with consequent loss of both the "I" and the world.

But obviously the hypothesis of *"Maybe one morning . . ."* is untouched by this revolution in technological per-spective. If the "usual illusion" is everything that lies before our eyes, then this illusion extends to that part of the ante-rior world which, in order to be framed in a mirror, claims to represent the posterior world, the world behind us. Even if the "I" of the poem were *driving* in an air of glass and turned around, he would see behind the car's rear window, not the landscape with its white stripe on the tar, the stretch of road just traveled, the cars he thought he had passed, but an infinite, empty abyss.

In any case, in Montale's mirrors—as Silvio D'Arco Avalle has shown for "The Earrings" (and "Pool" and other waters)—the images are not reflected, but emerge ("from below"), rising to meet the observer.

The reordering of the world occurs "as on a screen,"

and the metaphor brings the movies to mind. Poetic convention has traditionally employed the word "screen" in the sense of "sheltered concealment" or "diaphragm"; and there is, I think, little chance of being mistaken if we say that this is the first time an Italian poet has used "screen" in the sense of "a surface on which images are projected." The poem (dated between 1921 and 1925) clearly belongs to the age of the movies, in which the world passes before us like photographic shadows; trees houses hills extend across a canvas backdrop; the rapidity of their appearance ("suddenly") and enumeration evokes a succession of images in movement. We are not told that these images are projected; their *accamparsi* [reassembling] (meaning "to put into a *campo* [field]", whereas here the *visual field* is directly alluded to) might not refer to a source or matrix of the image; it might spring directly from the screen (as we saw with the mirror), but it is also the spectator's illusion that the images come from the screen.

Traditionally, the illusion of the world was rendered by poets and dramatists through theatrical metaphors; for the world-as-theater our century substitutes the world-as-movie, a rapid unscrolling of images on a white screen.

The poem contains two distinct rapid movements: that of the mind that intuits and that of the world that passes. To understand them is wholly a matter of being very quick, or of turning suddenly around in order to surprise the "hide-behind." This turning has a dizzying effect, and knowledge lies in that dizziness. The empirical world, on the other hand, is the usual succession of images on the screen, an optical illusion like that of the movies, in which the speed of the shots persuades you of their continuity.

There is also a third rhythm dominating these two, and this is the rhythm of meditation, the intense, suspended progress in the morning air, the silence in which the secret gathered in the lightning-swift intuitive movement is concealed. A substantial likeness links this "quietly [going] my way" to the nothingness, the void which we know is the beginning and end of everything, and to the "air of dry / glass," which is simply its least illusory external appearance. Apparently this "going my way" is not distinguished from that of "men who don't look back" who have also, each in his own way, perhaps understood, and among whom the poet ends by mingling. And it is this

third rhythm which, more gravely, resumes the light note
of the beginning and closes the poem.

Valmorbia . . . (undated)

One of the few poems related to M.'s experiences as an infan-
try officer on the Austrian front during the final years of World
War I. In 1917, after an officers' training course at Parma, M. was
dispatched to Vallarsa in the Trentino and put in command of a
forward post above the Leno river, near the village of Valmorbia.
Because he loathed violence and honored life in all its forms, he
was extremely reticent about his military experience. "If I had to
charge an enemy with fixed bayonet," he told a friend, "I'd have
been dead right away; even in those days I wasn't very quick.
Besides, I didn't hate the enemy, and I couldn't have killed either
man or beast. . . ." His attitude, he felt, was later confirmed by
events. One rainy night he was dispatched with his patrol to scout
enemy positions; on every side he could hear shells exploding.
Toward morning the patrol surprised three Austrian soldiers who
surrendered without a shot. Later, in the pocket of one of his three
prisoners, M. found a small volume of Rilke's poetry. For M.'s
own poetic memory of the event, see "L'eroismo" ("Heroism") in
Quaderno di quattro anni.

Like "Almost a Fantasia" earlier, the poem transforms the
hellish shell-pocked slopes of the Vallarsa sector into a scene of
idyllic Alpine beauty. The signal flares, like flowers, sprout on
their stems; a trench—or rather a foxhole—becomes a cave or grotto;
the night, whitened by flares and explosions, is a protracted dawn.
The entire poem, in short, reveals the power of memory to pro-
duce timeless "oblivion / of the world," a perpetual "half-light"
which, like all paradises, can create either an Eden (as here) or the
paralyzed torpor of life-in-death (as in "Wind and Banners").

The poem's densely worked texture, above all the way in which
M. here and elsewhere uses the phonic associations of proper names
to create subliminally effective meaning, is sensitively registered
by Almansi and Merry (37–8):

> Clearly the poem is dominated by the twice-repeated place-
> name (and portmanteau word) "Valmorbia," which encloses
> the resonance of a "gentle valley" *[valle morbida]*. The sin-
> gle word conveys etymologically as well as phonetically an

overriding impression of relaxed serenity. Even the other place-name, "Leno," accompanied by the matching bisyllabic adjective *"roco"* [hoarse] as though it were really *"lene"* [soft], intervenes to suggest a subdued gentleness of sound. There is, in this repetition of the first name in the poem, both times in strong position at the opening of a new line, a reinforcement of its own suggestiveness. In such a comforting location, the clouds do not simply pass over our heads, but they flow discursively by (*"scorrono"* and *"discorrono"*—they flow and chat with us all at once). They move with the same fluency as the words in the entire poem are marshalled to enchant us. . . . With the closing strophe, the main subjects (Valmorbia and the memory) return to their rightful position before the verb in the sentence: *"Le notti . . . erano"; "Valmorbia . . .* [era]." A talismanic power is given to the second occurrence of the name *Valmorbia* by presenting it almost tautologously for what it is—*"un nome,"* in a bounded parenthesis of its own. It seems to say: "Valmorbia, *only* a name," but in fact implies ". . . far more than a name," and as this name-*plus* fades in the last full-throated cadence of the poem—*"terra dove non annotta"* [land where there's no night]—memory itself and the thought of war die together with it, although Montale preserves the underlying ambiguity of his attitude to the sleeplessness: this may be a delirious consciousness induced by the softness of the whole scene; it may still be the nightmare of war which impedes any slumber.

Your hand was trying . . . (1924)

In manuscript, this poem was inscribed "to P." [Paola Nicoli], to whom "The Lemon Trees" was, "with brotherly good wishes" *[con un augurio fraterno],* first dedicated.

The young lady—not the poet's beloved but a friend (M. pointedly uses the polite *vostra* instead of the intimate *tu*—persists in trying *[tentava]* to sight-read an unfamiliar score. She is a skilled pianist ("the language most your own"), but unspecified sorrow causes her to stumble, striking out chords that express the "notationless" grief she feels. The poem's "I" is of course M., the poet who consistently distrusted poetry as evasion of life and an emotional artifice. Like the woman, he too is unable to find words which express his real feelings (cf. "The real tale belongs to men of silence" in *"I know that moment . . ."*). Frustration produces "blockade," a silence. But the silence is *shared:* at first with the woman, then with the scene framed in and beyond the window, which opens out *(varco!)* onto a vista of the wordless natural world— sea, sun, leaves, butterflies dancing in the light. Everything, man and woman included, merges in a music of silence, a *simpatia* that *precedes* words and which would be deformed by any language but this eloquent miracle of quietly shared ignorance. The break-through, like every such *varco* beyond the "fallen" world of lan-guage, lasts only an instant before being annulled by "ordinary reality" and deformed by notations—words, notes, images—fash-ioned in the hope of seizing the unseizable. But it is precisely these "flashes" that illuminate the world and on which memory there-fore so needily fastens. Life provides what poetry at its best can only hope to hint at and revive. But that revival first demands the poet's candid confession of the inadequacy of poetry and an effort to strip himself of anything that might impede recovery of that pure-hearted "ignorance" that is the (Socratic) condition of any knowledge worth possessing. This at least seems to be the impli-cation of M.'s famous eulogy of his dead friend, Sergio Fadin:

> Always to be among the first, and to *know,* this is what matters, even if the *why* of the performance escapes us. The man who has had from you this high teaching of *daily decency* (the hardest of the virtues) can wait patiently for the book of your relics. Your word was not perhaps of the written kind.
>
> ["Visit to Fadin," *The Storm and Other Things*]

The children's farandole . . . (undated)

M.'s familiar paradoxical *motif;* life emerges from death (where else can it come from?), the timeless moment from time, joy from sorrow, the divine from the human. The poem celebrates the sea-sonal miracle of rebirth, life exploding from drought. The faran-dole (Ital., *farandola*) is a dance deriving from the Auvergne and Provence; hands linked, the dancers wind along the streets or through an open space, in this case the "crucible" of the Ligurian shore. Once again M.'s human beings reveal their oneness with the natural world by assuming the semblance of plants (see "Chrysalis," "Shoot stretching from the wall . . .," etc.). But as soon as the identity is asserted, and the language expresses the thought, then alienation, the sense of being "far from his ancient roots," slices down like a knife, and the momentary Edenic miracle (when "even names, even clothes, were sin") vanishes, leaving merely another relic, another "cuttlefish bone," on the beach.

W.A.: *Far from his ancient roots.* A glance at Dante's Earthly Paradise (*Purg.* xxviii, 142): "Here the human root *[l' umana radice]* was innocent."

Faint wind-borne sistrum . . . (undated)

The disconsolate return to blockade after the preceding paradisal vision of children dancing is intensified in one of the bleakest poems M. ever wrote. The first stanza sets out the image of the cicada's dying music, a glancing metaphor (as in "The Shade of the Magnolia" in *The Storm*) for the poetic voice, solo and fading. The metallic, cicadalike chirr of the sistrum—the musically acute M. chooses precisely the right instrument—attenuates in the brown air (twilight? Dantesque limbo-light?) of a universal torpor. But, as the second stanza reveals, that same weak voice began as a surging spring, a "source" that branched out (see *"There Triton surges . . ."*), its network sustaining a feeble world incapable, it seems, of standing on its own. Such, once, was the magical power of poetry—a power capable (see "Almost a Fantasia") of invigorating, almost of creating, the world. But poetry, like the world it once sustained, has "fallen"; blockade is everywhere. Gesture, whether action or words, is wasted effort; it fills the darkening air of the third stanza with a quivering of vestiges, the relics of a life so spent that even the "void" (in the Greek sense of "chaos" as the primal matrix, the womb of miracle—see *"Maybe one morning . . ."*) cannot absorb them. The end is silence, as the vital energy that once surged into voice and action returns, stripped and bleak, to the source from which it came.

The windlass creaks . . . (undated)

The subject is once again lost love remembered, but also, more pertinently, the deformation of loving memory itself in the image of the beloved's once laughing face, now contorted and creased with age as the pail sinks into the black oblivion of the well. If the image of windlass and pail renews the past, it also intensifies the pain of separation and loss. As Dante's Francesca observes, *"Nessun maggior dolore / che ricordarsi del tempo felice / nella miseria"* ["No greater pain than to remember, in wretchedness, the happy time" (*Inf.* v, 121–22)]. It is added ironic pain that the image of the beloved is transformed as the years would have done, into "someone else," her features aged by the wrinkling water into which she sinks. With great deftness M. explores the modalities of memory. The rasping creak *[cigola]* of the windlass as it hauls up the brimming promise of the bucket, and then, with a screech *[stride]*, lowers it back to the depths, recreates the shock of memory suddenly surfacing and then abruptly vanishing, at the same time that the tenuousness of the image, the wavering features and evanescent lips, suggest the beloved's unseizability *[inafferrabilità]*. The idea, reminiscent of Dante's frustrated efforts to embrace a shade that, like smoke, evades his grasp, appears, never exactly repeated, throughout M.'s poetry. See, for instance, "Pool"; or in *The Occasions,* the image of the cable car in the motet, *"Flower on the cliff's edge . . . ";* or in *The Storm,* the escalator image of "A Metropolitan Christmas" and the ghostly visitation of Clizia in "Voice That Came with the Coots."

Haul your paper boats . . . (1924)

E.M., writing to Giulio Einuadi (Feb. 16, 1942):

> If the drafts of the ornery *Ossi* are still within reach, I'd like to request a correction . . . that is, in the twentieth of that series of "true and proper" "Cuttlefish Bones"—the one beginning *"Haul your paper boats . . ."* [*Arremba su la strinata proda . . .*]. In the last line the word *amarra* [draw on shore, i.e., to beach], which I changed to *ammara,* should (if possible) revert to the original word, *amarra.* The line should be corrected as follows:
>
> *Amarra la tua flotta tra le siepi.*
>
> [Beach your fleet, secure it in the brush.]
>
> In fact, *ammarare* means "to moor" and in 1925 I was certainly influenced by the Ligurian *amurrà* which means "to

beach," exactly what I wanted to say. Consulting the dictionary misled me. . . .

E.M., in a letter to Gianfranco Contini (Oct. 31, 1945):

By *padrone* [*"fanciulleto padrone"* in line 3] I meant the person who deals in small trading without being certified captain; so if you find something like "my little sea-wolf, my four-penny commodore," you'll be more on target. However, *padrone* [master] is a legally recognized title. . . .

This scrupulous attention to minute detail, so characteristic of M., is anything but finicky. Meaning lies in nuanced detail. A *beached* boat is drawn ashore; launched at the propitious moment, it is ready to confront the sea: a *moored* boat is fastened to man-made ballards or wharf-cleats. As always, M. chooses the interstitial point in both time and space for the frail craft of poetry and the precarious works of man: sheltered from the evil spirits at sea, but safe too from the perilous moment that threatens "months of toil" and the landward dangers from the walled orchard. Neither nature nor culture; neither-and-both.

Hoopoe, merry bird . . . (1924–25?)

The common European hoopoe (*Upupa epops*—derived onomatopoetically from its call, "a low, far-carrying *poo-poo-poo*") is a thrush-sized bird with barred black-and-white wings and tail. Its most conspicuous feature is its great semicircular erectile crest, bordered with white and tipped with black, resembling a medieval jester's cap. The crest is normally depressed but, when erect, opens and shuts like a fan, repeatedly. An early March visitor to Italy, he is regarded, like the cuckoo in England, as a "herald of spring." The hoopoe was first "slandered" (that is, represented as an avine clown) in Aristophanes' *Birds* (which in turn plays on Sophocles' representation of Tereus as a hoopoe in the lost tragedy, *Tereus*); but M. is probably referring to Parini, Boito, and Foscolo, in whose writings the hoopoe appears in an ominous, even sinister light.

Above the graffiti-covered wall . . . (undated)

Finale of the suite, this bleak little poem closes on a note of bemused resignation: *varco,* a passage seaward past the confining wall is apparently impossible (or possible only to those boats anchored in the bay). Impasse, it seems, is a permanent condition. The reprise of earlier images and motifs (wall, shards, vault or dome of the sky, waking mornings, etc.) is sustained by the familiar counterpointing of polarities: land / sea; blockade / liberation; finite / infinite; transient / timeless; necessity / miracle; workaday limbo / paradisal.

The poem's setting is anything but idyllic: an urban or resort waterfront consisting of wharves, anchorage, marina, a street with a large wall (a *muro* that becomes a *muraglia* in the third stanza) shading (at sunset?) a couple of benches. The wall itself is covered with graffiti, an image of human transience that is also intended (as M. once observed) to convey a sense of the city, of the "blockade" of everyday life. In pointed contrast, the phrase *l' arco del cielo* ("the vault of heaven") is a literary locution whose purpose is to evoke the grand celestial architecture, Ptolemaic and Dantesque, which it once designated. That ancient cosmos, as the stanza's final, one-word line *finito* so emphatically declares, is not only "finite" (limited) but is now "finished," "gone," "done for."

The second stanza extends the emphasis by cosmologizing the "blockade." What was once a vital flame (see note on "Sarcophagi") surging through the "veins" of a sentient universe is now nothing but shards: cold, lifeless abstractions (cf. "the bright air" in *"Don't take shelter in the shade . . .,"* where these ideal forms could still be glimpsed behind phenomena, and which are here irreparably broken and scattered).

The third stanza "comes to terms" with this reality. No sudden breakthrough into *varco,* merely a tonelessly patient acceptance of *noia,* the tedium of ordinary existence lived without expectation of "miracle." An ordinary new day opens onto a prospect of stale sights and all-too-familiar objects—wharves, wall, road—their banality conveyed by a long string of flat -a's: "banchine / e la muraglia e l'usata strada," etc. Hope of escape, if any, is very glancingly and negatively hinted by the sight of boats riding at anchor—that is, temporarily confined for now but capable of, and indeed built for, *varco* seaward. They are thus analogous to the faint but unkillable hope anchored in the heart of the observer—a hope that will be unexpectedly liberated by the joyous apparition or "sign" of the two blue jays diving seaward in the first poem of the great suite of "Mediterranean" that follows.

MEDITERRANEAN (1924)

Joseph Cary (259–65):

"Mediterranean" . . . is a genuine suite of nine parts which, as the name indicates, faces away from the baked and stony land towards the sea. "I am a tree burnt out by sirocco," Montale wrote to Svevo in 1926, apropos of the life expressed in the pages of his recently published book, and this is an image which in its desolation and suggestion of helpless capitulation to "superior" powers certainly corresponds to a major portion of the experience given by the poems. . . . [Elsewhere] Montale uses a different gathering metaphor: "In *Ossi di seppia,* everything was drawn and absorbed by the fermenting sea. . . ."

The sea indeed is the other aspect of riviera, experienced not only as "distance" or barrier but as Thalean *source,* a power in and through which change into something rich and strange is conceivable, *varco* and / or transfiguration a possibility. In the early [poem "Seacoasts"], for example, the sea is hailed as a Dionysian force bearing the individual beyond himself into some renovative communion with all Nature. In "Falsetto" the sea is Esterina's divine lover, reinvigorating and purifying the creature who dares its protean arms, though a mocking menace to the race of those who remain on earth. Doubtless part of what makes Portovenere a place of "origins" is its intimate involvement with the sea. But "Mediterranean" is Montale's major poem based on this dispensation.

The adjectival title modifies not just the sea but the speaker as well: he too is "Mediterranean" and must call the sea not only *antico,* ancient one, but *padre.* The suite begins and ends—as it must, spoken as it is by [him] who must finally remain on earth—with the rocky summer coast. At its opening, he lies in siesta on the ground, vacantly registering the sound of the waves along the shore. His reverie is broken by "a sound of strident jeers" and as he raises his head he sees two jays, feathered blue and white and with the speed of arrows, shoot toward the sea. No comment here: merely a happening or occasion which directs the *flâneur's* roused attention to the great presence beside him. And with this stagesetting event the poem's main movement begins: the high speech (eloquent, formal sol-

ranean speaking to the Mediterranean, which is given the *tu* as is right when that Power is fathering.

In the second section, the speaker recalls the "solemn admonition" breathed by the sea now as in summers long ago:

> . . . the pretty ferment
> of my heart was merely a moment
> of yours; that your perilous law
> lay deep within me: to be vast and various,
> but unchanging too,
> and so cleanse myself of every foulness.
> You showed me how. . . .

Here the speaker feels himself "no longer worthy" of that great lesson. Yet in the third section he recounts a recent vision in which the rocky shore that is his *paese* seemed to amorously consent and thrust itself towards the waters' "invisible embrace":

> O immensity, it was you, redeeming
> even the stones in their suffering:
> in your jubilation, the fixity
> of finite things was justified.

Now the speaker, standing in and allied with the finitude of rocks, is touched to joyous worship by this prospect of infinitely free power. Yet, this same "suffering of stones" provokes the main note of the fourth section where, from the thought of a city sunken beneath the sea that is suggested by the images of clouds reflected in the water, there comes the reminder of the "severe law" governing all finite existence (here called "nameless suffering turned to stone"): the implacability of process, of sea . . .

> . . . that chaos of debris
> hurled aside by the torrent of life

The fifth section broods on this opposition between power and impotence, exultation and suffering, infinitude and finitude, and so develops an exacerbated awareness of the cruelty in things. His life, he says, is a dry slope slowly crumbling away, or perhaps this plant . . . born in the

229

"devastation" of the careless pounding of wind and sea. He
is the daisy thrusting from a cracked soil:

> In this flower I tremble toward the sea that lashes me;
> silence is still an absence in my life.

Such "silence" of course would be the stillness of perfect
submission. At the end of the section, however, a sort of
"filial" yielding occurs—the speaker gazes at the peaceful
riviera scene presently before him and his poor rebellion
gives way to a rueful rephrasing of infelicity as "perhaps
the rancor that every son has, Sea, for his father." This
modification of personal defiance through the sheer pres-
ence of the fathering sea is increasingly apparent as "Med-
iterranean" moves to its conclusion.

In the sixth section, the poet meditates on heredity
(the experience of Liguria and the *Ossi di seppia*) in terms
of a voice transmitted from sea-father to son:

> . . . some small part of your genius
> lives on in these syllables we bear with us,
> humming bees.

Such an inheritance, speech with the savor of *sale greco* (sea
brine and / or Attic salt), is an apt enough description of
not only the saline flavor of irony that is present in so much
of Montale (e.g., in the *api ronzanti* who constitute the epi-
thet for poets in the passage above) but of the "Homeric"
resonance of which he is capable when he chooses—as, for
example, in the opening eight lines of section six, where
aulicity of diction and phrasing fully responds to the cere-
monial piety expressed.

Section seven returns to matters raised in section two;
that is, his "unworthiness" of the sea's example: to be vast,
manifold, and "fixed" or integral at once. Here the speaker
is aware that his perversion of the sea's qualities is a para-
lyzing sense of flux and disintegration—that he himself is
torn and dispersed through his perception of infinite pos-
sibilities of action: This section proceeds by a series of rhe-
torical alternatives: what he would like to be and what he
is or is not. Thus, he would wish himself to be "rough and
elemental," as integral as a pebble rolled in the sea, and
instead of this he is at once a consciousness of and identi-

fication with the fume of "fugitive life." In language and aspiration reminiscent of the vision of the infernal machine in *"I limoni,"* he would wish:

> . . . to search out the evil
> gnawing at the world, the little warp
> in the lever that locks
> the universal gears. . . .

But instead of this he is a helpless witness to the chaos implicit in each instant. Once, we recall, at Portovenere, to "decide" seemed stupid; now he could not decide if he wanted to. So the sea has been a bad master. But the section ends with a drastic change of heart similar to that of section five. The mere presence of the sea is conversional, finite consciousness is drowned:

> But I have no regrets: once more
> your song undoes my inward knots.
> And now your frenzy rises to the stars.

The same sort of resolution by drowning occurs in section eight, which resumes the subject of section six. But the certainty expressed in that section (that something of the sea would forever reverberate in his voice) is now known to be a dream. What, he inquires with bitter sarcasm, has such vital power to do with his sort of temperamental *senilità*, "my melancholy of an aged child who ought not to have thought"? Instead of the sea's *salmastre parole* (salty words), he has only *lamentosa letteratura*, the faded language of the dictionaries, words like public women (the witty Italian for this is *donne publicate,* published women). The final straw is to have even these "tired phrases" stolen tomorrow and integrated in a genuine poetry *(versi veri)* by studious *canaille.* The gamut of resentments here, the commonplace nature of his complaints and the ridiculousness of the final flareup about the *studenti canaglie* is extraordinarily rich and dramatic, and the modulation or shift at the end—again like section five and section seven—gains enormously in dramatic impact as a result of it. The agent of conversion is, again, the presence of the Mediterranean:

> And your booming grows, and the blue
> of the fresh shadow widens.

My thoughts fail, they leave me.
I have no sense, no senses. No limit.

The ninth and last section returns us to where we began:
land and [noon *(meriggio)*]. Ecstasy, even wishfulness, have
gone. In their place there is the grim clairvoyance we asso-
ciate with the *Ossi* group. The speaker now stands beside
what he felt as the fathering sea, now "like a muted mem-
ory when someone recalls his home," resigned to his tran-
sience and eventual obliteration "like an ephemeral scrawl
on a blackboard." His lesson from the sea has been learned
in this ["desolate noon"] in which the dream of *varco,* the
hope of in some way assuming or incorporating in himself
the sea's glorious energy, has evaporated. And so the
sequence ends in a capitulation, not so much to the sea as
to the sea's infinite difference, to the "wall" separating the
limited from the limitless:

> I commit myself to you. I am nothing
> but the spark of a thyrsus. I know it well: burning—
> this, and only this, is my meaning.

Perhaps that culminating *tirso* of which the speaker finds he
is only a byproduct provides a useful point from which to
appraise the qualities and originalities of "Mediterranean."
Primarily *tirso* is a "literary" noun, part of a standard poetic
lexicon where it means "thyrsus," the ivy-wreathed and
phallic staff carried by Dionysus and his followers. As such
it relates to one central thematic strand of the sequence,
the "filial" connection between man and nature (here the
fermenting Mediterranean). Under the sign of the thyrsus,
then, the speaker aspires to his source, to nature, and would
reject, if he could, his "face," his individualized and finite
self. According to the myth expressed in "Mediterranean"
the suffering stone is "redeemed" by the sea, and the
sequence reaches its climax in this direction as the speaker
feels his thoughts abandon him in a rush: *"Sensi non ho; né
senso. Non ho limite."*
　　And under the aegis of the thyrsus we are led to make
a curious connection between Montale's "Mediterranean"
and—of all possible predecessors—Gabriele D'Annunzio's
book of summer *Alcyone* (Halcyon). *Alcyone,* written in

1903 as part of the *Laudi* cycle, exhibits D'Annunzio's considerable talents at their most genial. The book purports to be a lyric journal of a summer spent in the coastal region just to the south of the Riviera di Levante. It begins in June and ends in September. As one might expect from this poet, the mood *passim* is ecstatic and dithyrambic. Creatures of the Dionysian dispensation, satyrs, nymphs, naiads, and so on, abound and are constantly evoked and embraced; the rhythms are ebullient and skillfully martellated to create an exultant and somewhat hypnotic effect. Stress is all on the sphere of physical sensation and the brake or "inhibition" of intellect or *coscienza* is utterly absent. We know that the D'Annunzio of this phase loved to ride horseback along the edge of the Ligurian Sea, galloping "centaurlike" at the foam lip between surf and sand, at the edge of another dispensation where, when the speed was high enough he could sense his unity with the world whistling around him and achieve an ecstatic communion with the scheme of things. He even reports a high point where he was thrown from his horse and, one foot still in the stirrup, dragged a certain distance down the beach. The dizzily dislocated *lido*'s-eye view he then had of the waves breaking on the shore was for him a spectacular epiphany.

The point of the D'Annunzian experience in *Alcyone*, then, is elemental—he loses his name, his historical and psychological identity, and becomes his environment. His style works to render this experience in dithyrambic terms:

> . . . and the river is my vein,
> the mountain my forehead,
> the forest my groin,
> the cloud is my sweat. . . .
> And my life is divine.

Accompanying this merger, votive offerings to the Graces, Bacchantes, and nymphs, aspects all of presiding Dionysus and his transforming thyrsus.

But such a *tirso* represents a very different thing in the world of [Montale's] "Mediterranean." For one thing, the sweeping consummation it represents is only momentary in the . . . sequence: an abolition or evasion of consciousness which, while it lasts, also abolishes the sense of limits.

And while it lasts this is felicity. But, the narrative movement of the poem reminds us, consciousness is only dispersed momentarily; one returns to oneself, "comes to" at a reformed wall. Even Montale's rhythms in this sequence—a kind of Italian "blank verse" grounded on an approximate hendecasyllable that can be expanded or contracted to fit the tempo of thought—suggest meditation and a highly speculative mind rather than any sort of dithyrambic release. (For example, despite the "D'Annunzian" climaxes of sections eight and nine—*Non ho limite,* etc.—not a single exclamation point.) . . .

But one other point should be made. [Montale's] staying, his burning, constitutes in itself a sort of witness: he becomes a sign and warning for others. And in this sense a commitment and relation *is* established—not with "nature" but with other men. Can it be called "sacrifice" when such an action (absence of action?) has no alternative, is in fact a sentence? Here intention is everything. This climactic *bruciare* that is the speaker's signification might, given the intention, be understood *not only* as hellish suffering but as vocation, as a service offered up to others who move "outward" towards some inconceivable *varco*.

NOONS AND SHADOWS

End of Childhood (1924)

Almansi and Merry (46–9):

The first of the three parts in ["Noons and Shadows"] opens with ["End of Childhood"], . . . the longest poem in *Ossi di seppia* and also the poem most deeply rooted in the author's past. [A. Seroni has] pointed out how it presents us with "a frankly stated ideal topography" of Montale's discovery of the world. First of all he sees a closed centre, "hospitable, defended from the outside, isolated and static in the face of the elements." Here the child takes up a position of ecstatic contemplation, his soul still unconscious of the "male di vivere" [evil of living]. Next the boy moves into a ["game with the outside world"]: Montale says . . . [that] "things became clothed with names, / and our world acquired a centre." This stage of "game with the outside world" . . . is a period when the horror of visions, the threat of a *pro-*

celloso evento [stormy happening], is suspected but as yet not understood. Finally, the whole of nature is explored and grasped as the permanent beckoning image of return to a place of peace and quiet typical of childhood. We would add that the poem is dominated by a sense of long duration in its imperfect tenses, which only give way to a sharper past remote tense in the seventh of its eight sections. . . . Thus the last two strophes of the poem stage the "ending" of the title by their very change in tense and mood, whereas a calm certainty was conveyed by the preceding imperfect in all of the opening six strophes. These verbs in the imperfect, always in Montale tending to be the tense of nostalgia, suggest the security of childhood and serene definition of the surrounding world. . . . The same process will be put in motion in the near-by poem ["Eclogue"], which bathes the poet's childhood in the soft glow of "Fine dell'infanzia." Both poems begin at the shore of the sea, then ["Eclogue"] gives way to the breaking of illusions by a different change of time, in this case to the present tense:

> Random
> thoughts came springing to mind
> in that air too still.
> Now the watered blue is gone.
> The family pine leaps out. . . .

["End of Childhood," however], . . . encloses a view on life as well as a view on childhood. The near-by "hills" and "olive groves," the "pathways" which lead back to the "house on the sea" or the roads which extend to recesses "covered in shade and silences," are all seen through the eye of a child but feared by the mind of an adult; for the poet transfigures them into barriers which again require a secret path or broken link to penetrate towards salvation:

> We rarely crossed the nearest ridges
> of those peaks; even now our memory, exhausted,
> lacks the courage to cross them.

The enormity of this challenge is conveyed both semantically and metrically here, with the long and solemn pause between *"monti"* and *"varcarli"* at the caesura of the second line quoted. The childhood peaks thus become *finis terrae* for Montale, and he will use this name for the first and most celebrated section of the third volume, *La bufera e altro*. The poet's memory tries to verify whether even childhood was dogged by the obsession with the broken link, or the crack in the universal machine, or the search for the passage or the vision beyond the half-closed door:

> a flickering
> alternation of strange realities,
> but governed by an elusive rhythm.

Instead, this childhood was closed off and protected by the salvation that comes from ignorance, and this notion was "stamped" forever on the poet's consciousness and is stamped on this text by the phrase which defines the greatest moment of optimism and hope in Montale's expression of the world:

> the cozy shelter
> of our wide-eyed childhood.

This formula, that cries out from the fifth strophe of the poem, seems to us as memorable and shattering an evocation of childhood as the celebrated line from Baudelaire, *"Le vert paradis des amours enfantines."*

AGAVE ON THE CLIFF (1922)

A lyric suite like "Sarcophagi," consisting of three movements, each devoted to a different wind and linked by the agave with which (or whom) the poet in the first poem identifies himself. (For the important and persistent motif in M. of "the human plant," see *"Suddenly, at times . . ."*—"In this flower I tremble toward the sea"—but also *"The children's farandole . . ."* and "Arsenio.") Physically, the setting is a Ligurian cliffside fronting the sea. Existentially, it is the liminal outpost of an undecided self whose conflicting spiritual impulses—confinement and immobility (expressed as earth-rootedness) on the one hand, and boundless free movement (sea, sky, birds) on the other—are set against each other in revealing dialectical tension. In this context the three winds represent the environing world, changing aspects of that "weather of reality" to which the conflicted self-as-agave responds and, by progressing from bud to blossom, defines itself.

Scirocco: oppressively hot, moisture-laden, southerly wind whose relentless blowing is both nerve-racking and debilitating. Here it functions as a dissolvent of reality, creating a chaos ("that seething / of every essence"): objects, events, and light, even time itself, become a jittery, unintelligible confusion in which will, identity, and purpose all disappear. The agave-as-poet responds with an ambivalence born of his nature and place. Earth-rooted and immobile, it flinches from the convulsive flurry of the sky and the gaping jaws of the sea, while at the same time it wants *not* to resist, craves to repudiate its roots and dissolve sympathetically with everything else in that chaotic *unisono* of nature which prevents the tightly budded agave from blooming and the torn "I" from winning an identity.

Tramontana: powerful, bitingly cold northerly wind—the antecedent of M.'s later metaphysical storm-wind, *la bufera* (see, for instance, the second and third sections of "Bellosguardo Times" in *The Occasions*). Unlike the dissolvent *scirocco,* the *tramontana* is "a will of iron," an alien force of different nature ("how alien they seem, these ghosts / that flash past") to which the slender agave must in order to survive resist with all the strength of its earth-hugging roots. (For thematic anticipation see the last two lines of "Falsetto"; for reprise, see the image of Arsenio as "a reed dragging its roots, all slime, / never torn up, quivering with life.")

Mistral: strong, cold, dry wind from the north—milder in Liguria than in the Rhone valley—always accompanied by brilliant sunlight and cloudless skies. In such favorable weather the poet-agave bursts at last into bloom, fully realized. But only momentarily. The expansive calm of sea and land prevailing in the first three (untranslatably rhymed and intricately assonant) stanzas is not shared by the agave, whose ambivalent nature—earth-rooted but sea-leaning and sky-aspiring—is metaphysically restless *(mia vita turbata),* discontented with its own rootedness when challenged by the seabirds soaring past with their migratory, transcendental injunction: "Farther!"

Pool (1923)

The Italian critic d'A. S. Avalle has argued that the chief theme of this dense little lyric is that of a defeated or blockaded memory.[1] Fraught with the promise of meaning, the memory attempts to surface to the mind of the rememberer; failing, it recedes, stillborn, to the depths below. This theme and its associated images link it, according to Avalle, to "*The windlass creaks* . . ." earlier, and to its full, final expression in "The Earrings" in *The Storm and Other Things*. Despite its interpretative richness and subtlety, Avalle's analysis is not, I think, wholly convincing. The argument, as Luperini has observed,[2] is vitiated by being based upon the 1926 version of the poem rather than the definitively revised 1942 version (from which M. cut fifteen lines or more than half the original poem). The result is two very different poems, which it would be critically improper, as well as misleading, to conflate.

If we stay with the text as revised in 1942 and refuse to allow the earlier version to influence our reading, then the theme of the poem can only be, as Luperini maintains, failed or defeated identity. The poem means what it seems to say: an unformed embryo of incipient life struggles vainly to emerge and "become," to acquire an individual name, then fails and sinks back, drowning into the undifferentiated life below. Such a theme obviously links the poem intimately to other instances of unrealized life or failed birth: to "Scirocco" with its "buds clenched tight / incapable of breaking into bloom," and to the "strangled life" *(vita strozzata)* of "Arsenio"; to the "drowned presence" *(O sommersa!)* of "Encounter"; or the "failed miracle" of the female figure in "Chrysalis"; and even to the agonizingly frustrated coast-haunting spirits of "The Dead," struggling to return to life.

But the poem says more, or says it more interestingly, than Luperini allows. The first two lines, for instance, are mediated by an (oddly undetected) allusion to Dante, and, through this allusion, they confirm and deepen the paradisal motif so tellingly sounded in "End of Childhood" and again in "Eclogue" and "Slope." If we read naturalistically, the setting of the poem seems distinctly strange: a man-made pool, suggestively formal, but

[1] *Tre saggi su Montale* (Turin, 1970), 32, 79, 82.
[2] Montale e l'identità negata (Naples, 1984), 69ff. See also Luperini's *Storia di Montale* (Bari, 1986), 46–7.

improbably edged by flowering belladonna (from Ital. *bella donna*), better known as deadly nightshade, hardly the ornament of choice. Behind this odd and obviously contrived setting, we—that is, educated readers of Italian—are surely meant to catch a glimpse of Dante's Earthly Paradise (*Purg.* xxviii) and the springlike apparition of Matelda, her arms full of freshly gathered flowers. There by the water of Lethe, Dante addresses her: *"Deh, bella donna."* She approaches, smiling from the other side of the stream *(Ella ridea dall' altra riva dritta).* Later, to Dante's surprise, she is still smiling "in this place chosen / for the nest of the human race." In sum, all the elements—*bella donna*, flowers, water, smile—item for item, of M.'s idyllic setting, in which paradisal felicity and time-lessness are suggested by the smile that brushes the tremulous, miraculous *now* of heaven-reflecting water. Then, as in "End of Childhood," the paradisal "instant of forever" is abruptly shattered: in "End of Childhood" by the "expectation of a storm," a wind kicking up; in "Pool" by a tossed pebble that cracks the glassy film of the water. In both poems the illusion of happy enclosure is suddenly and irreversibly revealed for what it is. Like the opaque forms in *"Above the graffiti-covered wall . . . ,"* the heavenly apparitions glimpsed in the pool are dispersed, and the wrinkled water becomes the image of time and history *(il tempo fatto acqua)* as in "News from Amiata" *(The Occasions)* and *"The windlass creaks . . ."* Fallen from Being into Becoming, the embryonic "I" flinches in shame from the Beatrice-like observer of his defeated struggle, though she has almost certainly been at his side from the beginning, smiling at him as Matelda smiled at Dante.

Eclogue (1923)

An important poem, too often dismissed as a simple "farewell to youth." Ostensibly a poetic contrast of *then* and *now*, it engages and inflects M.'s familiar polarities. Thus the child's "eternal instant" is set against the "fallen" world of adult time; silence is opposed to sound, the miracle to necessity, *varco* to "blockade." Thematically the poem looks back to "End of Childhood," "Almost a Fantasia" and *"There Triton surges . . . ,"* but it also glancingly anticipates the final poems, with their saving apparitions of female figures—"Chrysalis," "Delta," and "Encounter," and, still later, the great poems of *The Occasions* and *The Storm and Other Things* with their supreme angelic *donna,* Clizia.

The first stanza evokes the stunned world so vividly limned in "End of Childhood": a paradisal Ligurian noon, alive with tremulous olive trees, birdsong, and freshets. Like any Eden, this world and the childhood inseparably linked to it are doomed to pass: too good, too perfect, to last. Its air, as the pivotal last line tersely informs us, is "too still."

The second stanza accordingly begins with gradual dissolution of the idyll. As afternoon advances, the magical iridescence of "watered blue" (see note on "Moiré") fades into a grisaille of haze. Time now threatens, the illusion of permanence disappears: "all around / a lost hour sheds its chains." In "End of Childhood" the timeless "instant of forever" was dissipated by the expectation of a storm; here, the paradisal silence is shattered by a succession of discrete, everyday sounds: a train, a shot cracking "the glassy air," a flock of startled birds. The instant vanishes, burned away (*bruciata;* cf. "I know it well: burning— / this, and only this, is my meaning," from final poem of "Mediterranean"), leaving as its ashen residue the bitter memory of paradise lost.

But in M.'s world life survives in such residues. Hope in particular persists, a smoldering in the ashes of memory. And it is hope that quickens ("Soon the idyll can be reborn") in the third stanza. But the haze deepens, and the miracle fails to take place, expiring in the thickening blur of heat. For one tantalizing instant, however, a woman's figure flickers faintly in the scrub. But she is not the maenad or Bacchante who might have been expected to appear "in these Saturnalias of heat." Who is she then? We cannot of course be sure, but the shy or elided female epiphanies in such poems as "Delta" and "Encounter" suggest that her apparition belongs, not to the childhood world of undifferentiated (Dionysiac) being, but to the visionary world of adult self-making. In more literary terms, she belongs, like the savior-*donna* of *"In limine"* and later poems, to a (modified) Dantesque, not D'Annunzian, order of things, a presage of things-to-come: an evanescent "presence" and bearer of a very different "miracle."

It is her abortive apparition that explains, I think, the tone of disillusioned or deeply bemused detachment audible in the words of the "I" in the fourth stanza. Like the boy he once was, the remembering man returns to the moonlit thorn-brake *(tra i vepri)* to hear the prodigy: the whistling hares. Once he had returned home from daylong vagabondage in riotous union with Nature; but, sensing that the miracle has somehow vanished, he sets out to rediscover it in the wild scrub. Like the boy, the adult man also returns to his *paese* but, because he has changed, finds himself estranged, unable to recover the old ecstasy. What he seeks in the moon-lit scrub is not the boy's prodigious hares but the vision of the woman briefly glimpsed in the afternoon haze—an apparition (like that of *"In limine"*) that summons him to "advance," to emerge and *live*. If the poem is a "farewell to childhood," it is that of a man who stands, diffidently conflicted, at the threshold of a *vita nuova*. Behind him, potent in memory, is the idyllic world to which he can no longer return; before him is the world to which his future calls him and which he regards with desire but also apprehension, feeling perhaps unequal to its ardors and that his failure may (as in "Pool") cause the vision to be withdrawn.

Flux (1924)

Like "Eclogue," a contrast of then and now, past and present, lived life and remembered life. Structurally, the poem is divided into two parts, two perspectives, each capped by a differently bleak judgment of existence. The first is based upon a succession of unrelated items or "instants": trickling brook, trembling elders, droning of bees, flotilla of paper boats, an arrow impaling a post. Elsewhere, in a different context, these instants might have coalesced into anticipatory "signs" of "the miracle"; here they are simply items in a random, indifferent "now," incapable of cohering into meaning. Life, in short, as detritus: a desultory profusion of merely banal objects and events: "more futile than / cruel." Continuity is provided by the boys who return "every minute, every season." In the second part the perspective of the returning boys is set against that of the adult man making his return to the same events, the "vivid shards" of a past indelibly limned in memory (just as in "End of Childhood" the sight of a man on a mule "was stamped forever on that laundered / blue—and etched in memory too"). But, like the hoped-for "miracle," the past is irrecoverable. Disillusioned and estranged, the man glimpses a world of total flux, full vision of which he sympathetically transfers to the greater experience and ruthless candor of the venerable statue of goddess

Summer (a glance perhaps at the statue of the snub-nosed Seasons—*Le Stagioni camuse*—in the garden of Guido Gozzano's "Signornia Felicitá"). Herself a vandalized (i.e., enduring but destructible) image of time *sub specie humanitatis,* not *aeternitatis,* knowing that she is ultimately as doomed as everything else, the goddess shrinks into the encircling ivy as though shielding herself from the injury of absolute time, the (Heraclitean) flux or cyclical torrent of Life ("more cruel than futile")—a torrent that overpowers everything in a "chaos of debris," statues and paper boats alike, and plunges for that abyss which Dante calls *lo gran mar de l' essere* ("the great sea of Being").

Very different interpretation, however, is provided by Silvio Ramat in *Montale* (Florence, 1965), 65–6:

> "Flux" (or "Flowings") is of an artistic quality quite different [from that of "Eclogue"]. It too is linked, rather more closely, to "End of Childhood" and to other poems as well. Once again (for the third time) we see boys intent on launching paper boats (the same words used in the "Epigram" for Camillo Sbarbaro), while the theme, rather more severe, recalls *"Haul your paper boats . . ."* But generally we can say that in all the poems of "Noons and Shadows" encountered up this point, we are involved with poetry of generous, perhaps benevolent memory. Even in a composition like "Flux," which has its moment of apparent agitation (in the flux of all things in "the great descent" which causes the foundering of "the little schooners . . . / in riptides of lather"), the feeling is one of tranquil vision, a feeling strong enough to reverse the meaning intended by Montale's own conclusion ("and life is more cruel than futile"), and leaving us with the more vivid impression of life as defined at the close of the first section ("this squandered waste / of everyday events, more futile / than cruel"). In addition, the "statue of goddess Summer" dominating the hill (which immediately summons up the memory of "the statue in the drowsing noon" *["I have often met . . ."]*) appears to be the image of a blander, more realistic indifference, quite unlike "the divine indifference" with its illusory comfort and false good. And there is no perceptible sign of cruelty in the details: "the blur of a blue dome." the sluggishly flowing brook, the accidie, the repose granted by the stars to the "poor wretches / who walk the white

roads" (an Arsenio-like expression *ante litteram*). The "droning of bees" is quietly natural, and the "squandered waste" seems not to have been preordained in some *alto loco* above us. Sluggishness does not mean poetic vacuity. Montale has rarely been so fastidious and so pointed. He knows, for instance, the secret of making stones speak and of cloaking the pilotless "little schooners" with an aura of adventure. The return of the boys in a domain which is no longer that of time (and to which only the statue is infallible witness) is a device for arriving at the prediction (positive, I believe) that "someday / the cycle that governs our life / will guide us back to that distant past, / its vivid shards printed / on curtains that do not stir / by an unknown lantern."

Slope (1924–26?)

In a note to P. Gadda Contini, M. set forth his motifs. Chief among them was the Ligurian countryside, which he described as being both "extremely universal" and "at times hallucinated but often naturalistic." Few of M.'s landscapes are more hallucinatedly universal than that of "Slope." A few physical details (eroding cliff, sea, sunlight, a possible cicada) support a bleak metaphysical geography and the darkening of an existential day. "My life," M. had said in "Mediterranean" V, "is this dry slope *[clivo]*." The focus in "Slope," however, has been widened to include a vision of man's life as dissolution and declivity from youth to age, strength to weakness, boundless hope to defeated acceptance. The day dawns with a fanfare of trumpets expressive of the brash vigor of the early light and youthful hope undimmed by memory. The geography is elemental: transient earth confronts eternal sea. At their mutual frontier, the cliff, these two overlapping but incompatible "orders" meet and collide. Like the storm-lashed agave earlier, the cliff stubbornly resists the onslaught of the sea, here too the daimonic manifestation of an infinite, timeless order. The "word" that plunges from cliff to gorge is the voice of the eroding cliff, the very sound of earth dissolving—transience enacted—on the breakers. The challenge that it trumpets to the sea is possible, however, only to the vaulting confidence of youth, a fact forgotten or unimaginable in the bright morning world, memoryless in the overpowering promise of the day.

In the blazing heat of the dangerous hour of noon, hope and confidence, like the imagined world itself, shrink ("the end is certain now"). A shrilling cicada (the timelessly undying voice; see "Eclogue": "only the grave cicadas can endure / in these Saturnalias of heat") scrapes away "at the chain" whose links presumably "bind us" to the causal structures of ordinary time and reality. In the second strophe, the landslide is universalized. Certainties dissolve, individual forms, identities, objects crumble, almost it seems with a relief of defeat. Rooted things dig in. Paths on the cliff collapse as hands grope for purchase. But struggle is futile. As the day wanes and darkens, a different "order"—the undifferentiated world—descends. And just as in "Flux" an ordinary summer stream is swallowed up in the seasonless "great descent" of Heraclitean flux *(panta rhei)*, so here the undifferentiated eternity of the background (night, sea death) swallows up the transient foreground (earth, day, life). The effect is the total shattering of the chains filed by the rasping cicada in the first strophe. Freed of "limits"— liberated, that is, from individual forms and identities—the persons and things of the visible world sink resignedly, almost with the relief of defeat it seems, into the dark blank of the abyss, where they become one with the night, the crumbled cliff, and the sea.

Throughout the *Ossi* the temptation to immerse oneself or drown in an underwater nirvana persists. But never until now has the pull of negative transcendence on a life-weary world been rendered more apocalyptically, with a deeper sense of absolute defeat, than here. Simply compare, for instance, the ecstatically reverent hymn, all balance and good health, of contentedly differentiated morning-man addressed to the sea, the great undifferentiated "other" of "Mediterranean" III. There too the cliff with its boulders confronts the sea: "Hard matter intuited / the approaching gorge and quivered, / and the tufts of the reeds, eagerly / swaying, spoke assent / to the unseen waters. / O immensity, it was you, redeeming / even the stones in their suffering: / in your jubilation the fixity / of finite things was justified." In contrast, "Slope" ends, not with trumpets but a dissonant animal *ululo* (squalling, howling), the keening horns of defeated life. The world *cielo* (sky, heaven), as Cambon has without exaggeration observed, "touches off the *Götterdämmerung* of *sfacelo* [undoing, ruin]." This word closes the poem. Accented on the antepenult, it pointedly refuses closure and produces an aposiopesis in which the poem, like the cliff it describes,

crumbles away, disintegrating into the abyss and whatever, if any-
thing, lies there or beyond it. It is into this abyss that Arsenio, a
man drowning in the tenuous hope of living, if only in the life of
another, now makes his descent.

Arsenio (1927)

E.M.:

The oldest poem in the book—*"To laze at noon . . ."* etc.—
belongs to 1916; the most recent—"Arsenio," to 1927. The
arrangement of the lyrics is more or less chronological only
in certain groups, but the various groups should be regarded
as parallel. . . .

★ ★ ★

I didn't think [at the time of *The Occasions*] of pure lyric in
the sense it later had amongst us [in Italy] too, of a play of
sonorities; but rather of an end-result which had to contain
its themes without revealing them, or rather without flatly
declaring them. Granting that in art there is a balance
between external and internal, between the occasion and
the work-as-object, it was necessary to express the object
and mute the provoking occasion. A new non-Parnassian
way of immersing the reader in *medias res,* a total absorp-
tion of intentions in objective results. In this also I was
driven by instinct, not by theory (I don't believe that Eliot's
theory of the "objective correlative" existed in 1928 when
my "Arsenio" was published in *The Criterion* [in an English
translation by Mario Praz]).[3] In substance, it doesn't seem
to me that the new book *[The Occasions]* contradicted the
results of the first *[Cuttlefish Bones]:* it eliminated some of
its impurities and tried to attack that barrier between inter-
nal and external which seemed to me insubstantial even
from the epistemological point of view.

—"Imaginary Interview" (Sulla poesia, 566–67)

[3] [*Stanley Burnshaw provides a useful history for this charged phrase:* " 'The phrase was formu-
lated by a half-forgotten classicist, Washington Allston,' says Harry Levin, *Context of
Criticism,* Cambridge, Harvard University Press, 1957, p. 259. 'Eliot himself was sur-
prised when he learned about the origin of the phrase . . . But the actual phrase comes
from the lectures on art, posthumously edited by R. H. Dana and published—as I remem-
ber—around 1850' (p. 16). —Personal letter to me. See also Bruce R. McElderry, Jr.,
'Santayana's and Eliot's "Objective Correlative," ' *Boston University Studies in English,* III,
1957, pp. 179–181." Stanley Burnshaw, *The Seamless Web* (New York Braziller, 1970,
75). —*R. W.*]

The poem, rightly regarded as one of M.'s most sustained and powerful, even in its extraordinary bleakness, has produced extensive critical exegesis. Here, somewhat abbreviated, is that of Almansi and Merry (49–52):

> The great poem "Arsenio" . . . is a difficult and obscure poem, inhabited by menacing symbols, ominous presences: the "rolling rumble of a thunder-sheet," the "silent roll of the gypsies' kettledrums," the reed which drags its viscous roots along with it, against which the speaker is explicitly compared, and the crest of an antique wave which rushes him along until, in the closing line, a strangled life which "rose" for him is carried off "with the ashes of the stars." Praz and other commentators clearly identify the poet himself as the figure of Arsenio, self-centered and solitary, and the location as a sea-side resort on the Ligurian coast of Montale's childhood. C. Scarpati notes how the indecisive nature of Arsenio recalls the "devitalized" characters in Svevo's novels, to which Montale was the first writer to draw critical attention in the 1920's. Praz sees a grey, lifeless routine of the poet's day being instantly disturbed by the "sign of another orbit" introduced at the opening of the second strophe. Following this critic's reading, the elements are seen as coming alive at this point: a water-spout is crossing the sky, the poet moves, in order to feel the gravel crunch under his feet; he makes at least one positive act by trampling into the "tangle of seaweeds" [il viluppo dell' alghe]. But the ending of the strophe is again pessimistic, and must close off whatever excitement was detected by Praz:
>
> > . . . link
> > in a chain, unmoving motion, ah, that too familiar
> > ecstasy, Arsenio, of inertia. . . .
>
> There is a passage in Montale's "Imaginary Interview" where the poet says that in these years, under the particular influence of Bergson and Boutroux, "miracle was for me as evident as necessity." He goes on to state:
>
> > . . . a thin veil, hardly a thread, separated me from the final quid. Absolute expression would mean the

tearing of that veil, of that thread: an explosion, or else
the end of the delusion of the world as representation.
But this was an unattainable end.

Is the miraculous break-through possible? At the begin-
ning of the third and fourth strophes Arsenio urges himself
to make the effort in the imperative, but these commands,
involving a weird synaesthesia, suggest the depressed air
of Ligurian sea-side entertainments out of season. . . .
The crisis in the poem is solved by a sudden rain-storm,
washing out and muddying the edge of tension which traps
the protagonist:

> . . . until the sky
> shivers into drops, and the dank earth steams,
> everything around you spills over, the drooping
> awnings flap, a huge flurry
> brushes the earth: hissing,
> the paper lanterns fall soggy to the streets.

In the whole history of Italian poetry from the Trecento
onwards, it is hard to find any other poet who could trans-
form an unpleasant day-to-day occurrence into a cosmic
drama with such a symphonic crescendo of histrionic and
lyric effects. The last lines of the strophe quoted above would
never have been possible without the mediation, for
example, of such poems as the Baudelairean *"Voyage"* or
Rimbaud's *"Bateau ivre,"* which orchestrate a lyrical intui-
tion in a composite dramatic discourse. Here French sym-
bolism is the crucial intermediary between the original
sources (above all, the ever-present lesson of Petrarch) and
the new poetry.

In the final strophe the poet becomes a reed, weaker
and more provisional than the *"roseau pensant"* of Pascal
. . . carried along inside the flood and the collapsing awn-
ings. Inside these temporary surroundings from his child-
hood memories, the poet is reclaimed and nailed back to
the "frozen multitude of the dead." The poem thus ends
with a rejection of the Romantics' pathetic fallacy, as Praz[4]

[4]For Praz's commentary, see *The Poem Itself,* Stanley Burnshaw, ed. (New York, 1960),
319–21.

247

points out. There can be no sympathy from the tawdry
sea-front lanterns, and the miracle of expression embarked
on in the first section of the poem has transposed itself into
the kiss of death. In the last strophe Praz sees the poet as
"painfully alive to this one awareness of death, beyond the
reach of any human succor—that faintly heard voice is soon
carried by the wind, and made remote as the memory of a
dead universe."

> . . . and once again
> all things seize you, street, arcades,
> mirrors, walls, fixing you in a single
> frozen multitude of the dead,
> and should one gesture graze you, one word
> fall at your side, perhaps, Arsenio,
> in the hour dissolving, this is the call
> of some strangled life that emerged on your behalf,
> and the wind whirls it away with the ashes of the stars.

Forti finds that the poet has never gone so deep into him-
self, endowing the expressible (but more significantly, also
the inexpressible part of himself) with form. However, the
"delirium" at the end of the second strophe, and "stars"
placed at the end of the fourth, should remind us of the line
"un astrale delirio si disfrena" [a delirium is unleashed among
the stars: from "Moiré"], and the conclusion of "Mediter-
ranean" VII: *"il tuo delirio sale agli astri ormai"* [and now
your frenzy rises to the stars]. The connection between
"astro" and *"delirio"* in all such locations creates an emphatic
and one could even say euphoric combination in Montale.
There is no doubt that the ending of "Arsenio" is a desper-
ate one, with the vision of a cosmic wind that dispels into
the void the last remnants of all human vicissitudes together
with an apocalyptic star-dust. The poet is employing a
visionary vocabulary to revel in the drastic nature of his
defeat. The astral delirium sensed by the reader in the close
of this poem provides a hinting analogy with previous
contexts where the writer is comforted by the minute
manifestations of nature in the wind and the sea. It seems
to us that the last line of "Arsenio" is redeemed by some
of the panic glory of his earlier moments. Montale's "white,
bleached" hero (for this is the etymological meaning of the

title)[5] looks up at the storm and the stars with some of the confidence that comes from the desolate purity of cuttlefish bones.

Chrysalis (1924)

The most searching account in English of this powerful poem is that of Cary (268–72):

> Once again we are in an *orto,* a small domestic orchard. It is April, new leaves and flowers appear from moment to moment, the warm wind—as in *"In limine"*—bears life with it in waves. But here things are more gnomic. In the prefatory poem the characters were two: the speaker-counsellor who might be the poet, and you, *tu,* possibly the reader, anyway someone addressed in restrained but intimate emotion.
>
> In "Chrysalis" the speaker has recognizable connections with [the speaker] of *"In limine"* in his bitter sense of the ironies of a springtide which may bring renewal to others but not himself. He stands, a meditative onlooker, in a "dark corner" of the garden, repeatedly associating himself (verbally) with shadow. He thus seems a "vegetable shade" in the Dantean sense, peering on the living (spring, "you") with a mixture of resignation and envy from what he calls his "squalid limbo of maimed existences."

As the poem develops, his presence takes on a darker, "sicker" note:

> You are my prey: you offer me
> one brief hour of trembling human life.
> Not one instant would I lose:

[5] Almansi and Merry appear to derive "Arsenio" from the compound root *arseno-,* whence *arsenico* ["arsenic"]. Though ash-white in color, *arsenico* can only by stretching things be translated "white, bleached," and thereby linked to the "desolate purity of cuttlefish bones." M., always interested in galvanizing the latent etymological energies of words, would, I believe, have wanted the reader to link the grayish-white quality of Arsenio's nature and name to the "ashes of the stars." (The word "arsenic" is, curiously enough, derived from the Greek word *arsēn,* "male," "man.") Even more urgently present perhaps is a connection between *Arsenio* and *arso,* the adjectival past participle of *ardere,* "to burn," and, in that *ars-* of *Arsenio* the ironic echo of the famous last lines of the last poem in the "Mediterranean": "I know it well: burning, / this, and only this, is my meaning." [W.A.]

His contemplation thus has its succubic or vampirical side—the speaker "preys" upon the life-energies about him. As the poem amply illustrates, even the pangs involved in spring's renewal have their value to him as being symptomatic of real life, prized by one for whom even pain has become routine.

The "you" is not the customary *tu*, but *voi*, a plurality. The main function of such pronouns is to lend the discourse the dramatic immediacy associated with the vocative, and *who* exactly is spoken to often seems of minor importance. Always, of course, the vocatives work to bring the reader into the story, and the *voi* of "Chrysalis," like the *tu* elsewhere, assuredly covers each and every one of us perusing Montale. But beyond this, *voi* seems to refer here to the myriad aspects of burgeoning natural life within the garden, a kind of Aprilic composite or coalition fermenting about the staring shade:

> These are yours, these scattered
> trees, moist, joyous,
> revived by April's breath.
> For me in this shadow observing you,
> another shoot greens again—and you *are*.

But this life also involves specifically "human" features. At one moment in the poem "you" are transfixed by a memory and a sudden sense of time's rapid passage, and the "human tremor" that betrays this event is watched, almost gulped, avidly from the shadows. At another moment "you" seem infected by the grim despair of the witness or spy you are probably quite unconscious of, and then you are "reclaimed" by the shade who sucks you into its own despair:

> . . . even your rebirth is a barren secret,
> a failed miracle like all the others
> who flourish at our side.

Now "you" and "I" become "we" as gradually the relation revealed in the first third of the poem (life and light scrutinized by death and shadow) blurs into common depression. We look out to sea at this point, observe its mists and clouds "shaped like a schooner" and in conscious self-irony fantasticate upon our approaching salvation:

> . . . in the sultry noon
> the sloop of our salvation appears, heaves to
> (see the water churning in the shoals!)
> then sprouts a boat that rocks
> in the gentle swell—and awaits us there.

This detailed "hypothesis of Grace," enunciated in sarcasm, constitutes the cruellest moment of the poem. At this point the speaker turns in a shudder of revulsion from his own contaminating bitterness to a simpler, less contorted expression of his suffering. And here the *voi* is given a summary name—*crisalide,* butterfly-in-the-making with its promise or future of flight. The name reestablishes original distinctions between those who stay and those who move out, but for the moment the general destiny is contemplated in terms already familiar to us:

> and we will go doggedly on, never moving
> one stone in the great wall;
> and perhaps everything is fixed, the script written,
> and we will never see, rising on our way,
> freedom, the miracle,
> the unnecessitated act.

With this evocation of *varco* the final movement begins; the tenderness implicated in the climax-vocative of "Chrysalis" is realized through a pledge of substitution-sacrifice such as ended *"In limine."* The poem's concluding image even recapitulates the burning sign *(tirso)* of "Mediterranean." The speaker makes his "pact with destiny,"

> . . . to redeem your joy
> with my condemnation.
> This is the vow that is born again in me
> and afterwards will stir no more. I think then
> of those silent sacrifices that sustain
> the homes of the living; of the heart that renounces
> so a child may laugh, unconscious of the cost;
> of the clean cut that slashes through, of the dying

251

fire that quickens in a withered stalk
and shudders into flame.

So in the setting of an April garden by the sea a conversion
of a sort occurs. Alternately a psychic rape is conceived,
initiated and ultimately relinquished or sacrificed. But to
speak of mild sea, budding plants, warm breeze, shard,
chrysalis as "setting" obscures a central characteristic of
Montalean vision: the fact that there is no hard and fast
bounding line to be drawn between a consciousness and
the world it inhabits. "Everything is internal and every-
thing is external for today's man, without the so-called world
being necessarily our representation," he writes in [his essay,
"Imaginary Interview"]. "I do not know up to what point
the external world (the non-I of the philosophers) includes
or excludes my physical person." Such a notion as the phe-
nomenological "bracketing" *(epoché)* of Husserl—the intel-
lectual operation by which some *quid* of life can be separated
out and mounted in parentheses as a "pure" object for
study—would be, for Montale, comic were it not for its
disastrous social consequences. The self, the "I," is inextri-
cably bound up in what we call its "environment," sur-
rounding conditions. And hence it follows that the most
satisfactorily precise view of man will have to be specific,
even dramatic—in Montale's phrasing (italics his): "not the
individual, then, but *this* individual, in *this* place, in *this*
situation."

The matters touched upon here are not remote from
"Chrysalis" and the development of Montale's poetry after
Ossi di seppia. The "I" of "Chrysalis," for example, is not
presented as a more or less stable entity upon which other
entities press or impinge, but as a consciousness in contin-
uous flux and process. It can be defined only from moment
to moment, *"this* individual . . . *this* place . . . *this* situa-
tion"; it has no "definitive" or final identity except in terms
of its continually shifting relationships with presences and
conditions edging its very local jurisdiction. It acts and is
acted upon; its motions involve an astonishing range of
rhythms and vocal modulations covering the starts, feints,
shifts and realignments it lives through until the moving
and heroic coda, its formulation of a "pact." "Chrysalis" is
the dramatization of the fortunes of a consciousness mov-
ing from an obsessional and lacerating sense of its own

impotence to a commitment, *nevertheless,* to the well-being of another; a dramatic aria—if one wishes—of an evolving *coscienza.* In both theme and dramatic richness it anticipates the major work to come.

Moiré (1925)

Etymologically derived from *mare* (sea), the Italian title-word *marezzo* means "marbling" or "watering," a marblelike or wavelike effect produced by means of irregularly striated colors or markings on a neutral background; also an iridescent ripple-pattern in fabrics, i.e., moiré or shot silk. M.'s method in this sea-drenched book is to energize the etymon.

"Moiré" is an intricate *tour de force,* as thematically dense as it is formally elaborate, which harkens back to two *Ossi brevi,* "Don't take shelter in the shade . . ." and "Splendor of noon outspread. . . ," and, in its own "Noons and Shadows" section, to "Arsenio" and the final stanzas of "Chrysalis." Thematic conversation, as well as variations are maintained through the familiar contrast of land / sea, transience / eternity, dark / light, mobility / immobility, the world below *(quaggiù)* / the world above *(lassù).* Thus, in *"Don't take shelter . . ."* the poem's kestrellike *tu* is urged not to seek shelter in the thicket of the cane-brake ("stricken as though with sleep") and instead to risk the Dantesque heights, soaring upward toward the "one certainty," the blazing light of an absolute Noon. To these contrasting terms "Moiré" adds a contrast implicit in their very polarity—that of equilibrium, of balance won and balance lost. Thus the poem's first line—"You bail, the boat already lists" *(Aggotti, e già la barca si sbiliancia)*—suggests a doubly threatening balance: the boat lists, and the bat-haunted grotto is disturbingly dark. So dark that it requires a corrective light. The rower accordingly "adjusts," his companion bailing while he heads out toward open water and the light. The sequence, the reader will already have noted, involves a reprise of M.'s most persistent motifs: a barrier or blockade (the cramping walls of the cave) and *evasione* or *varco* (breakthrough from darkness to light).

Outside it is noon, full *meriggio,* the sun directly overhead. And now a new imbalance is felt. "Too much light," as in *"Splendor of noon outspread . . . ,"* confounds by dissipating all shadow, inducing a physical torpor but also a transcendental rapture. The oars of the boat lie slack in the oarlocks while memory and desire, vectors of individual identity, are adjured not to disturb the spell of this timeless noontide. Later, in the eleventh stanza, the rower's (presumably hesitant or reluctant) *tu* is urged to let her name "splash, sink / like ballast in water," i.e., to jettison that individuality that for M. is conveyed by the possession of a face and a name (see the last line of "Pool" and note thereon.). By so doing, the individual or differentiated self vanishes, melting into the Undifferentiated, the world of pure, sheeted Being represented by the absolute *meriggio* of this and other poems. In this world everything—forms, objects, shadows—dissolves into an iridescence of powdered light: "a shimmer of dust, / mother-of-pearl" in *"Don't take shelter . . ."* and in *"Splendor of noon . . ."* a light that turns everything into "a tawny shimmer." Thus, in Schopenhauer (an important and neglected influence in M.'s earlier work) the shattering of the "principle of individuation" (likened to a frail boat in a heavy sea) gives immediate access to the world of the Will that lies behind the illusory veil created by the World-as-Representation.

In any case, for M. the effect of the absolute Noon on those susceptible to its spell is attenuation or even dissolution of personal identity, which yields in turn to transcendental rapture or ecstasy. In the stillness of this sunstricken ecstasy (compare Arsenio's "too familiar / ecstasy . . . of inertia"), enfolded by "swarms and soarings," purpose, resolution, and "thoughts too lonely" (i.e., too individual) disappear into what M. in the crucial eleventh stanza of the poem calls an *astrale delirio* (astral delirium). If *astrale* here is taken in a Dantesque sense, as I think it should be—i.e., as a reference not to the stars generally but rather to *the* star, the sun, then *astrale delirio* will mean "passion for the sun" or "solar frenzy" (a phrase that recalls M.'s transcendental sunflower "crazed with light" and the closing lines of *"Don't take shelter . . ."* To this rapture the poem's speaker—a transparently Montalean persona—is all too susceptible. Indeed, the very lability of his persona is evident in his failure throughout the poem to make use of the pronoun "I," as though, like a man in love, his identity had already vanished, or were struggling to vanish, into the greater reality / identity of "you" and "we." In any case, what we know of him is largely conveyed by the way in which he courts his companion's complicity, urging her to share his ardor and rapture. But again and again his words betray a sense that this paradisal *varco* is as elusive as its bliss is brief. Thus in the seventh stanza, as though trying to sustain his *delirio* by the thought of its opposite, he somberly reflects, "Everything will roughen soon, / the waves darken with whiter stripes." Try as he will, he cannot erase the awareness of time *(il sentimento del tempo)* that persistently erodes his rapture. "Let your brimming heart dissolve," he urges his *tu*, "in these waves yawning wider," as though her "brimming heart" could somehow quell the roughening water. Only for the child (see "End of Childhood") is the miraculous "instant of forever" *(quella / eternità d'istante,* as M. will later call it), safe from the menace of time, and even then it is troubled by a vague awareness of things changing—a wind kicking up, a slope crumbling, a sudden darkness or void. For the grown man the miracle—whether in love, thought, or poetry—is as rare as it is precious, requiring of its seeker not so much luck as the possession of a second, adult innocence born of patience, endurance, and a knack for coping honestly with one's lived contradictions.

The evidence for this is not only the poetry but M.'s own words. "For me," he remarked in an interview, "the miracle was as manifest as reality. Immanence and transcendence aren't separable, and to make a state of mind out of the perennial mediation of the two terms, as modern historians propose, doesn't resolve the problem, or resolves it with an optimistic wave. We need to live our contradictions without evasions, but also without enjoying it too much. . . ." Immanence is lived *quaggiù,* "down here" in the everyday world of transience and change; transcendence is the life of *lassù,* lived "up there" in the solar radiance of the eternities. In human existence these polarities mingle without fusing, making a moiré or marbled pattern whose veins darken or lighten according to the time and weather of experience (e.g., "Everything will roughen soon, / the waves whiten with darker stripes").

Man himself is a moiré or *marezzo* variously veined dark and light by the contradictions—above all, that of immanence and transcendence—woven wavelike in his nature. At most times in most men and women these contradictions, though differently weighted, are dialectically linked: mutually, dramatically, reactive, and suddenly changing their patterns with unpredictable kaleidoscopic effect. Thus in the eleventh stanza the speaker's "solar frenzy mounts" but in the next line the ecstasy is recognized for what it is—*un male calmo e lucente* ("a malaise, quietly shining")—

a strange ecstasy that combining both rapture and awareness of the cost of such rapture—a subtle complexity of feeling only possible to a (Montalean) veteran of transcendence. But the point is essential both to the poem and the book as a whole. The ecstasy of what M. has elsewhere called "the transcendental I" is not only risky but destructive, a light that in M.'s words, "carries us toward a non-individual, and therefore non-human condition." (For elaboration of the point, see my introduction to *The Storm and Other Things*.) The triumph of either polar extreme—immanence or transcendence, dark or light, evil and good—would mean obliteration of that moiré that makes us both individual and human.

The final stanzas of the poem return the poet and his companion, saddened but still dazed by the afterglow of their "solar frenzy," to the world of time and immanence. The spell is broken; they feel the sudden weight of their own bodies; their very voices sound strange. But even while acknowledging that they are unchanged, i.e., not what they hoped to be (*non siamo diversi,* "we're no different"), the poet (transcendentally) urges his beloved to share his "ecstasy of inertia" and to sink down with him into a nether oblivion, the thickening sea-blue stasis or Nirvana of the abyss.

For a compelling but somewhat different reading of the poem and an extremely valuable account of the complex and powerful theme of *mer-riggio,* see Nicolas J. Perella, *Midday in Italian Literature* (Princeton, 1979), especially pages 240–62. The extraordinary lexical and syntactical richness of M.'s poetic style, as exemplified by the first two stanzas of "Moiré," has been closely and persuasively analyzed by the Italian critic Pier Vincenzo Mengaldo in his brilliant study, *La tradizione del novecento* (Milan 1975), 92:

> The design of the situation is wholly Montalean. Casual, familiar movements, pallid and tonally flat but at the same time tacitly menaced or apprehensive, are disposed in unrelated succession pointedly stressed by sentence syntax. Note the clear, sharp division into four periods, corresponding almost exactly to the metrical division into couplets; observe too the marked asyndeton between sentences, with the sole exception of the conjunction beginning the final period which simply introduces a closing cadence. Note also the poverty of the connective links within the periods: in the first period two coordinate conjunctions ("and" . . . "and"), both designed to slow the period; in the other

periods, the least subordinate conjunction—the relative *che*—
monotonously repeated. Actions and objects are accord-
ingly of a common everyday kind: water bailed from an
ordinary boat, a cave, a swarm of bats, an oar, a wall. For
the most part the diction is adapted to the objects; the phrase
S'è usciti marks a turn toward colloquial syntax, etc. The
very first word—*Agotti* (bail)—is at once technical and lit-
erary; the verb *si smeriglia* (loses its sheen), which governs
the metaphorical content of the second line, is technical but
also literarily elegant, and the effect of their combination is
to enrich and refine the literary image and at the same time
particularize it with almost scientific precision. . . . Simply
compare the phrase *cristallo dell' acque* with its conceivable
equivalents: *le acque di cristallo* or, worse, *le acque come cris-
tallo.* . . . [M.'s] dislike of any lush, idyllic vision of the
landscape and his demotion of it to everyday terms is,
however, . . . qualified by the rare and extremely literary
locution, *rancia* (orange). This word (Dantesque in origin,
as its pairing with [the colloquial] *sbilancia* makes clear) is
placed in a strong rhyming position and additionally involves
enjambment—the first of three such in eight lines. The agent
of the [colloquial] verb *scompiglia* (ruffles) is a [literary] *zefiro*
(zephyr), while the following line has its own aulicism in
[the literary] *anzi* rather than [the colloquial] *prima.* The
quite commonplace swarm of bats is split into its two
component parts by an extraordinary reversal of the usual
word-order; technically speaking, the oar "sounds" *(scan-
daglia)* the shadow, but instead of striking *il muro roccioso*
[normal usage], it strikes *il roccioso muro;* the rhyming—
alternate rhymes followed by cross-rhymes—is regular and
complete with a notable prevalence of harsh and unusual
pairs by turns assonant and consonant *(-ancia, -iglia, -aglia);*
on the other hand, it is accompanied by words deftly com-
bining literary and / or technical usage with colloquial (or
colloquially technical) usage. Finally, lexical elements of
diverse extraction and elevation are employed equally or
varied for important expressive effects (see above all the
repeated, parallel series of vigorous verbs beginning in *s,*
all placed at the end of the line). The result is that colloquial
and / or prosaic terms are joined to poetic and / or literarily
elegant ones, and, by combining what they least share—
on one hand, precise and exacting meaning; on the other,
objective particularization of individual phenomena—they

reciprocally define and specify, with a brilliance and clarity often bordering on hallucination and visual distortion.

House by the Sea (1925)

Almansi and Merry (56–9) comment perceptively, if not exhaustively, on this great poem:

> "Casa sul mare" . . . is usually seen as standing at the dividing-point between the different seasons of Ossi and Occasioni. Its title has already occurred in Ossi di seppia, as part of the text of "End of Childhood": "But those country paths brought us home / to the house by the sea, to the cozy shelter of our wide-eyed childhood." It looks forward to the menacing interiors of Montale's later poetry, as well as back to the seashore of his autobiography. The incisive and peremptory opening ("Here the journey ends") is followed by the matching opening of the other three strophes in the poem, all suggesting that a season and a whole experience have come to an end. Once upon a time [in "Wind and Banners"] Montale was able to write that "time never shapes its sands / the same way twice." Now, at the other end of the volume, Montale is complaining about an opposite oppression by time, and a few poems earlier, in "Arsenio," he inveighed against "the taut weave / of hours too much alike":

> Now minutes are implaccable, regular
> as the flywheel on a pump.
> One turn: a rumble of water rushing.
> Second turn: more water, occasional creakings.

The rumble of the water brought up by the pump, with its occasional creaking (cigolio), is reminiscent of the short Osso, "The windlass creaks . . . ," but here the water effects are subordinated as a long simile designed to convey the monotony of time. The overall purpose of the simile, as Valentini has observed, is to suggest the infallible mechanism of time and its inevitable progress parallel to the despairing journey in the composition. This water pump is a functional symbol; the pump in "The windlass creaks . . ." was first a presence and a physical fact, then a symbol. Thus the sound-effects produced by the revolutions of the

pump's wheel: *"Un altro, altr' acqua, a tratti un cigolio . . ."*
are constructed as three ineluctable slaps of water which
come no less equal and fixedly than the obsessiveness of
time from which neither Montale nor his interlocutors can
escape: *"UnALTR—"; "ALTR—ac . . . ; "a—TRAtti. . . ."*

The second strophe takes up at the shore of the sea.
This beach stands for the final stage of one journey and the
outset of another, one that may never take place. Yet the
shore which marks this considerable divide is itself cor-
roded:

> Here the journey ends, on this shore
> probed by slow, assiduous tides.

Life itself is therefore threatened by the marine messages:
here we have the apparition of two islands among the clouds,
called "migrant islands of the air," elsewhere the presence
out at sea was a schooner (in "Chrysalis"), the whistle of a
tug-boat ("Delta"), the acetylene lamps of scattered traw-
lers ("Arsenio") and the alluring call of the breakers. . . .
Before the spectacle of the sea, man is faced by the same
alternative as in "Falsetto": to stay on land or to choose an
elusive freedom and sail out toward the open sea:

> You ask: Is this how everything vanishes,
> in this thin haze of memories?
> Is every destiny fulfilled
> in the torpid hour or the breaker's sigh?

To the finite itinerary of a human destiny consummated in
passing whiffs of memory, the poet contrasts the wildly
improbably salvation of the willful companion:

> . . . transcendence may perhaps be theirs who want it,
> and you, who knows, could be one of those. Not I.
> There is no salvation, I think, for most,
> but every system is subverted by someone, someone
> breaks through *[passi il varco]*, becomes what he wanted to be.

In this passage the difficult *varco*. . . . is being crossed by a
privileged human being, even if it is qualified by the heavy
weight of a "perhaps." Yet the passage is an arduous one:

Before I yield, let me help you find
such a passage out, a path
fragile as ridge or foam
in the furrowed sea.

Once again—and we think back to Esterina in "Falsetto"—
the marine adventure may possibly represent a salvation,
but it is fraught with danger, with this fragile escape route
in the midst of a rough sea. The companion may take the
risky ticket for an unlikely eternity, while the poet accepts
the lulling quietness of a finite death:

My journey ends here on these shores
eroded by the to-and-fro of the tides.
Your heedless heart, so near, may even now
be lifting sail for the eternities.

The internal rhyme and assonance in Montale's description
of this shore *(che Róde la Maréa col Móto altéRno . . .)* with
its lullaby effect, pacifies the poet's restlessness. And in any
case he can never be the willful hunter after infinity, while
again a passage from the nearby poem "Arsenio" confirms
that the speaker is reluctant to finish any journey at all:

. . . maybe
this is the moment, so long awaited,
which frees you from your journey. . . .

★ ★ ★

W.A.: *does spiny Corsica or Capraia loom, / through islands of
migratory air.* "According to legend, the promontory of Portofino
is thought to be the farthest frontier of the living, from which can
be seen, floating in the distance of the sea, the Island of the Blessed.
This may be a rationalized reference to Corsica, which on very
clear days can be seen rising from the sea." *Guida all' Italia leggen-
daria* (Milan, 1971), 311.

The Dead (1926)

The dead, as the final *si sommergono* indicates, are "drowned"
or "submerged" existences. Metaphors of immersion and / or sub-
mersion occur frequently in preceding poems, but there are marked
sea-inflected differences. In "Falsetto," for instance, Esterina, like

a Ligurian Venus Anadyomene, surfaces, invigorated by immersion in her natural element, the breakers. In "Pool" a stillborn "life" struggles in vain to emerge as an individual from the undifferentiated depths of the pool. Arsenio–Montale is "a reed dragging its roots," a "descending" man swallowed by "an ancient wave." The *tu* of "Moiré" is adjured to let her heart "dissolve / in these waves" and her name sink "like ballast" in the water. In "Encounter" the numinous female figure is apostrophized *("O sommersa!")* as though she were in fact dead, a drowned presence. And in the following poem, "Delta," the poem's *tu* is a "stifled presence" *(presenza soffocata)* both in the poet's life and in the torrent of time, which has absorbed her individual / personal "time."

According to the *sommerso* who narrates the poem, the dead yearn to return to the land of the living—represented as a Dantesque "opposing / shore"—where they were buried, presumably one of those Ligurian cemeteries situated, like Valéry's *cimetière marin,* on a patch of high ground fronting the sea. In M.'s poetic eschatology, these dead share the defining passions of the species, itself conceived as a consortium that includes not only the living and the dead but variant forms of the "strangled life"—i.e., the living dead, the timid or defeated Limbo shades, existences unlived or unrealized—whose individual differences are all annulled in the community of universal "shipwreck." Like the living, these dead *sommersi* know the bitter frustration of "blockade" and lifelong imprisonment behind a "sheer wall" (see *"In limine"*), in their case the barrier of the opposing shore and that "icy stasis" that holds them, like the seabird tangled in the net, "motionless, migratory." No less than the living, they long for *varco,* liberation from limit and their present condition. Indeed, in M.'s thought, the craving for *varco* appears to be instinct in the species at all times and in whatever condition, a restless metaphysical discontent as innate and unkillable as the habit of (tenuous Montalean) hope.

What motivates this craving is the inextinguishable blaze of life itself ("I know it well: burning— / this, and only this, is my meaning"), smoldering on in the "lives" of the dead. The very nature of life is change and transmutation; it seeks to "go beyond," obedient to "the cycle that controls our life," in search of a fulfillment beyond the trammels of a given existential phase. It is life as an invincible, transcendental passion, by nature revolting against seaweedlike passivity, which seethes in the restlessly thrashing dead:

> . . . whatever in us
> was resigned to limit, by one day stilled,
> now seethes; between the strands weaving
> branch to branch, the heart thrashes
> like the gallinule
> trapped in the meshes
> where an icy stasis holds us,
> motionless, migratory.

For these (apparently recent) dead, *varco* means passage back to the warm embrace of human memory and the life once theirs. But the mesh of their condition tightens around them (cf. *"In limine"*), and the desired *varco* eludes them. Everywhere barriers and meshes—the wall of the opposing shore against which the sea crashes; nets drying in the late, cold light; even the cloud-stripes (?) of the storm-lashed *(flagellato)* horizon—confront and frustrate them. Then, their struggling flights baffled, they too—like Arsenio ("Descend . . . Descend . . ."), the landsliding cliff of "Slope" ("from the sky / plunging to the shore"), and the stream of "Flux"— join the "great descent" to the abyss. Even here, however, they are confronted by still another mesh, the *crivello / del mare* (sieve of the sea). Most commentators maintain that this final mesh represents the ultimate defeat of the dead, through which no *varco* is possible. On this view the poem is of course not only funereal but apocalyptically so. Alternatively, the sea's sieving action may be seen as purgatorial and to that degree positive, permitting at least partial or selective *varco*. In "Mediterranean," for instance, the sea appears as an eternal scavenger, the agent of universal process, tirelessly sifting the transient phenomenal world and casting up on the land the debris of existence: "every foulness," flotsam, trash, cuttlefish bones, "sea-wrack starfish cork, all / the waste of your abyss." This detritus is rejected, but whatever energies contribute to "the cycle that controls our lives," presumably pass through the meshes of the sieve. The reliquary, as in *"In limine,"* becomes a crucible.

Thus, for the dead, passage through the sieve may represent *varco* to a new condition, a transcendental metamorphosis which M., in a later poem, will term a *nuovo balzo* (new leap) to a new condition. The *Ossi* and later books suggest the operation in M.'s poetry of a pre-Socratic or Ovidian–Dantesque sense of Life: con-

tinual eclosion, metamorphosis, transhumanization. In this pro-
cess no quantum of vital (burning) energy is ever lost. What is lost
is the lifeless excrescence trapped by the sieve—husk, coating,
sheath, sloughed skin, bony residue, powderings, everything that
has temporarily enclosed a completed developmental phase of life.
This, at any rate, is the apparent implication of poems in *The Occa-
sions* and *The Storm and Other Things* (see "Voice That Came with
the Coots" and my note thereon). That the *varco* of "The Dead" is
also, though less explicitly, based upon such a notion of process
is, I believe, confirmed by the final aposiopesis—those three dots
trailing away after *si sommergono*—here and elsewhere M.'s way of
expressing the continuity of ongoing life-process, which it is beyond
the power of poet or poem to complete. Transhumanization *(tran-
sumanar)*, as Dante observed *(Par.* i, 70), "may not be expressed in
words." Closure is neither possible nor desirable.

Delta (1926)

This intensely, almost impossibly concentrated lyric appears
to be at once a meditation on memory-as-vision and on the nature
of a life (the poet's but also ours) not so much unlived as parasitic
upon, i.e., lived with and within, the life of another. (Cf. "You
are my prey: you offer me / one brief hour of trembling human
life" in "Chrysalis.") The "other" is the poem's *tu,* a *donna* of
miraculous, memorial apparition, endowed by the poet with pro-
digious, indeed almost angelic, power of life. An unacknowledged
co-presence immersed in the great torrent of life from which she
draws her formidable energies, she in turn, by means of secret
transfusion, nourishes the poet's life. (These transfusions, we might
translate, are those mysteriously powerful exchanges of height-
ened and heightening spiritual energy that link human beings,
inspiriting and, at times, transforming them.) But the torrent of
life is inseparable from the rush of Time, and the *donna* is the
memory of a presence that "descends" from some unknowably
dark and presumably eternal realm—from death and beyond death,
to the remembering poet at the liminal point (a threshold both
spatial and temporal) of the delta or "mouth" where the torrent
meets the sea. With her she brings a silted message or "sign," the
memory-news of what appears elsewhere as "another orbit," i.e.,
a different, higher *order* of existence, which she summons her

rememberer to seek and claim as his own. An apparition from the past, she is also (and perhaps therefore) a prospective savior, a guide to the future. In her are manifest then those energies of life intensified to which the poet aspires while timidly dreading the challenge she poses. She therefore (?) fails to appear or appears only as the "sign" latent in the whistle of the invisible tugboat making for port. (We should note the important fact of the urban setting here and in "Encounter.") In the opacity of this "sign" and setting the poem closes, its wan hope to some degree confirmed by the memory of "the sloop of salvation" in "Chrysalis" and the failed appearance of the expected savior in "Encounter."

Alvaro Valentini (*Lettura di Montale: "Ossi di seppia,"* 1971, 193–95) provides interpretative paraphrase:

In the everlasting flow of life, the poet finds himself bound to the woman at his side. In language both passionate and abstract he tries to tell her this:

Physically, life expresses itself [*si rompe,* "breaks out," a synonym for other Montalean words, e.g., *sgorga,* "gushes," "wells up"] in transfusions and crossovers which are also secret (and as such heighten the mystery of particulars and of general existence). It is this life which I have joined to you, even though, in its immensity, energy, and suffering, it seems unaware of personal events, even unaware of you, as though you were a presence suppressed by the cosmic machinery.

But in those moments when time, torrent-like, backs up, blocked by the dams of memory, you adapt yourself to its vast operation. And, like memory, you break into bloom, revealed from that dark, mysterious region whence you descended to me. In these moments an existence is not so much realized as heightened: as in fact, after the rain, the green of the trees and the cinnabar on the walls seem heightened.

Having descended from some dark, mysterious region, you are therefore mystery yourself. And, apart from your message, you are whatever of you flows into me, the life-courage you give me. Of you I know nothing at all. I don't know . . . whether you are a real presence or an imaginary one; whether, as vision, you were created in the haziness of a dream by the bank of a feverish torrent which . . . races turbidly and, at its mouth, crashes into the rising tide.

I know nothing of you in the wavering, uncertain hours, grey with boredom or unexpectedly rent by sulphuric flashes (caused by the miners' detonations). All I comprehend of you (or preferably: in relation to you) is the whistle of the tug looming from the fog as it makes for the harbor, since you too descend to me from some dark region. And you are my landfall too . . .

No doubt about it, a difficult poem: especially obscure in its closing relational statement which, understood as I suggest, might shed light on the preceding lines. That the lyric . . . anticipates *The Occasions* is undeniable, but we need to understand in what way. It is not enough to say that the second person addressed by the poet emerges indistinctly from memory and preserves a secret existence from which comes merely the hint of a silent message, and that the dialogue remains a monologue. To my mind the interesting point is that, in the fatalistic round of existence, in the prison of the hours, alongside the wall that cannot be crossed, perhaps no longer hoping to find *varco,* a break in the meshes of the net, or salvation in another orbit, the poet accepts the message that sustains him in life. Accepts it with a religious feeling, perhaps with the certainty that, by so doing, he lives in the soul of another: the woman he loves. The interpretation is strengthened if we bring to it one of M.'s later observations in *The Occasions:*

> Too many lives are needed to make one.
> ["Summer"]

—a statement clearly intended not in a purely physical sense . . . but in the more obvious psychological sense of a man who needs to see himself reflected in eyes that reassure him.

Encounter (1926)

Alternative titles were: (1) *"La foce"* (Mouth [of a river or torrent], i.e., the place where the torrent "encounters" the sea); and (2) "Arletta," the name of a girl, a childhood friend of M. who died young and whose wraithlike presence recurs throughout M.'s poetry, early and late. "A genius / of pure nonexistence," as M. will call her in a late poem, she dominates "Chrysalis," "House by the Sea," and "Delta," as well as "Encounter."

For discussion of the Arletta or Annetta figure, see Jared Becker, *Eugenio Montale* (Boston, 1986), 41–5. "Encounter," as Becker observes,

> portrays Arletta as a disembodied soul floating in an eerie, almost hallucinatory landscape that could well have been lifted from Dante's *Inferno*. The narrator finds himself confined to this underworld, feels himself encircled by *"impallidite vite tramontati"* and *"visi emunti, / mani scarne"* ("pale, darkening lives" and "sunken faces, / emaciated hands.") With the kind of helpless desperation that afflicts one in a nightmare, he struggles to locate the woman, trying to assure himself that she always hovers nearby to comfort him. But she never incontrovertibly materializes, until in a strange epiphany he convinces himself that she lurks in spirit form within a pathetic little plant growing on the doorstep of an inn. He stretches a hand toward her, and Daphne-like, she fluctuates for an instant between human and vegetative shape. Then, abruptly, she vanishes again.

Cary (273–74) provides helpful interpretative comment:

> The fourth section of "Mediterranean" had evoked the image of life as a "torrent" moving toward the sea, casting aside in its course the detritus of used-up individual lives. This amounts to a "philosophy." It is present everywhere in the poems now added to *Ossi di seppia:* in the "descent" of Arsenio from what could be the *corso* in Rappallo to the sea breaking in a summer storm, in the expiring of the ghosts of both the living and the dead on the "iron coast" in "The Dead," in the very title of "Delta" with its sense of silted deposits thrown up in ditches where the river meets the sea. The second stanza of the great "Encounter" places it with a fierce eloquence of which no other contemporary poet has been capable:
>
> *La foce è allato del torrente, sterile*
> *d' acque, vivo di pietre e di calcine;*
> *ma più foce di umani atti consunti,*
> *d' impallidite vite tramontanti*
> *oltre il confine*
> *che a cerchio ci rinchiude: visi emunti,*

mani scarne, cavalli in fila, ruote
stridule: vite no: vegetazioni
dell' altro mare che sovrasta il flutto.

[Where the river meets the sea, its mouth
is arid waste, alive with limewash and stony rubbish—
but more a sluice for the trash
of human acts, of wan, twilit lives setting
beyond the horizon
whose circle walls us in: emaciated faces,
bony hands, horses filing past, screeching
wheels—not lives, no, but vegetation
of the other sea that straddles this.]

The voices arising from this fluid cortège are full of suffer-
ing, prayers, curses, complaints. For the speaker, there is
only his sorrow—"sole living portent in this swarm" and
he begs it to stay as a kind of talisman of vital resistance
(like K.'s suffering or the maddened sunflower) against the
gathering blankness. Its precarious actuality momentarily
seems to attract other life, a submerged copresence—kin to
the *voi* in "Chrysalis"—which might bring nourishment
and the strength to defy: "To it I hold out my hand, and
feel another life make itself mine." Then it fades. But in
the brush with another life, what was "elegy" has been
transformed into the will to endure and, if possible, to con-
clude with integrity. What follows is one of the few radiant
moments of the *ventennio nero:*

Poi più nulla. Oh sommersa! tu dispari
qual sei venuta, e nulla so di te.
La tua vita è ancor tua: tra i guizzi rari
dal giorno sparsa già. Prega per me
allora ch'io discenda altro cammino
che una via di città,
nell' aria persa, innanzi al brulichio
dei vivi; ch'io ti senta accanto; ch'io
scenda senza viltà.

[Then nothing more. O drowned presence, you disappear
as you came, and I know nothing of you.
Your life is yours still, dispersed now
in the fitful glintings of day. Pray for me then,

pray that I descend by some other road
than a city street,
in the violet air, against the teeming tide
of the living, that I sense you at my side,
that I go down,
unflinching.]

★ ★ ★

W.A.: *the other sea that straddles this.* Commentators have generally interpreted "the other sea" as the sea of life, perhaps synonymous with Dante's *"gran mar de l' essere."* But it is important to distinguish between sea and torrent, here and elsewhere employed as an image of ordinary time (see note on "Flux")—time that sweeps away the detritus of human acts, residues of lived life, to its mouth where it meets the sea, i.e., encounters eternity. "Great rivers are the image of time," M. will write in "The Arno at Rovezzano" in *Satura.* Just as the Ligurian landscape is here both physical and metaphysical, so torrent and sea, in the basically Idealist landscape of M.'s poetry, possess the same duality.

in the violet air (nell'aria persa). The key word here is *persa,* which as past participle of *perdere* means "lost," an apt epithet for the infernal air. As an adjective, *persa* (from *persiano,* "Persian") is of Dantesque provenance (see *Inf.* vii, 89: *"Visitando vai per l' aer perso"*), and is used to indicate the color of Persian cloth, ranging from reddish brown to purplish black to gray verging on indigo. My rendering "violet" leans upon T. S. Eliot's hallucinatedly hellish rendering of this Dantesque word in "The Waste Land" ("And bats with baby faces in the violet light . . .").

Seacoasts (1920)

Unusually accessible, this lovely poem, one of M.'s earliest, requires little or no analytical commentary. Thematically, with its repertory of the book's dominant images and ideas (blockade and breakthrough, living-as-burning, arrowing birds, sunflower, torrent, dissolution, even cuttlefish bones), it reads as though it were a recapitulative coda expressly composed to unify the work. Its apparent structural motive is to provide a positive, dramatic resolution to the overpowering sense of impasse and apocalyptic "descent" created by the poems of the preceding section. And, for the most part, critics have tended to fault, not the poem itself, but rather the poet's strategy in employing an early work to resolve later poems of greater complexity, power, and moral import, manifestly resistant to comfortingly "upbeat" conclusions. Despite its undeniable beauty, the buoyant affirmations of "Seacoasts," and the fervent injunction to "a soul no longer divided" to "change elegy to hymn" and "make yourself new," have seemed radically out of place after the great dirge of "Encounter," the spectral vision of "The Dead," and the nightmarish Ligurian resort-world of "Arsenio." Admittedly, M.'s negatives, as in "The Dead," contain (usually very tenuous or modest) positive charges, and the poet's principle is obviously one that applies to overall structure as well as individual poems. Certainly there can be no doubt that the poet's purpose in rounding off the book with "Seacoasts" is to suggest a dialectical link between its exuberant optimism and the desperate *inabissamento* or "bottoming out" of the final poems of the "Noons and Shadows" sequence. But the contrasts are too great and the enjambment too sudden, the synthesis too much a papering-over of the problems, for the poet's strategy to effect belief. This, at any rate, appears to have been M.'s own view of the matter, who in "Imaginary Interview" remarked that the *Ossi* contained poems that "departed from my intentions . . . and lyrics (like "Seacoasts") that constituted too premature a synthesis and healing." In still another interview, he observed wryly that " 'Seacoasts,' the poem most preferred by the incompetent [critics], is the epilogue to a poetic phase that never existed. Which is why they have never managed to place it critically: in fact the *Ossi,* which it closes, don't permit such a conclusion."

Helpful discussion of the modern Italian poetics of childhood as related to "Seacoasts" is provided by Jared Becker, *Eugenio Montale,* Twayne (Boston, 1986), 45–51.